Wakey, Wakey, Rise and Shine

Unleash Your Power to Manifest the Life You Desire

By Daniel Warwick

For permission requests, please contact the author at: **beyondreality800@gmail.com**.

To Helena and Cicely, 'my love for you is infinite'

Who Is This Book For?

Have you ever felt like life is running you instead of the other way around? Do you find yourself tangled in everyday drama, constantly reacting to what's happening around you, and wondering if there's more to life than just keeping up?

This book is for you—the dreamer, the sceptic, the seeker, and the go-getter who's always on the move but rarely finds time to pause and reflect. It's a guide for anyone ready to step off the treadmill of life and take control.

Here's the truth: you have the power to master your own reality. Everything you've ever dreamt of—the peace, the purpose, the joy, the abundance—is already within your grasp. You just need the tools to unlock it.

This isn't a book filled with hard-to-digest science or obscure philosophical jargon. It's a practical, eye-opening journey designed to help you take charge of your life. You'll discover how to quiet the noise, focus on what truly matters, and align yourself with the infinite potential that lies within you.

By the time you turn the last page, you'll have the knowledge and confidence to create the life you've always wanted, on your terms. If you're ready to stop merely surviving and start thriving—let's begin.

About the Author

I was born in the early '60s in North London, the youngest of three siblings—Sarah, the eldest, and Ben, in the middle. Life was anything but ordinary. One day, out of the blue, or so it seemed to me, I gained another older sister, Lindy. My parents had adopted Lindy before Sarah was born, but I wasn't aware of her until I was about three or four as she was usually away at boarding school, a place for girls from tough backgrounds. I only saw her during school holidays.

My parents also fostered children from broken homes—mainly Black children—so our house was a buzzing, ever-changing hive of activity. Some kids stayed for a few weeks, others for years. It was cramped, chaotic, and a bit of a madhouse, but somehow, it worked.

My brother and I had the kind of free-range childhood that would give modern parents heart palpitations. We were out from morning till dusk, exploring, playing, and getting into all kinds of scrapes. Life was an adventure, and despite the occasional bumps and bruises, we navigated it with curiosity and resilience.

I was generally a happy kid but absolutely loathed school—apart from art and football, which I loved and excelled at. Senior school was a dreary Victorian building, cold and uninspiring, and most lessons felt like a form of torture. One teacher even smoked through every class, filling the room with a fog thick enough to rival an old '70s working man's pub. My school reports were equally uninspired: "Daniel tends to stare out of the window, gently dozing." In reality, I wasn't dozing; I was daydreaming about being anywhere but there.

My saving grace was football. Despite being small, I was lightning fast and earned the nickname Wizard of the Wing at my local club. But at 16, the moment the final school bell rang, I bolted out of there at the speed of light. It felt like a jailbreak. Everything changed when I went to art school and was finally allowed to pursue my passion for creativity.

After leaving art school, I unknowingly began harnessing the power of manifestation. Within just two years, I had built a professional recording studio to pursue my passion for music, leading to the release of three self-penned albums. My journey then expanded into the world of film, and before long, I found myself running a million-pound facility, fully funded by investors who had backed my music. I never questioned how these opportunities unfolded—I simply expected them to appear, and they did.

Life hasn't been without its challenges—there have been plenty of ups and downs, dramas, and moments of doubt. By my early 30s, I was driven to understand more about reality and how our choices and intentions shape the world around us.

However, thinking back, the real turning point came when I was around 11 years old. Out of nowhere, a question struck me with such force that it kept me awake at night: *Why does anything exist at all?* Not how does it exist or what exists, but why?

It wasn't just a fleeting curiosity—it felt like an existential crisis wrapped in a riddle. And yet, when I shared my musings, my mother would brush it off with, "I've no idea what you're talking about. Haven't you got something better to worry about?" But, no—I didn't.

I also began to notice something strange about myself. The part of me that was aware of being aware didn't feel like the same 11-year-old boy running around in this life. It felt like there were two of me: the little boy, living out his story, and this quiet observer in the background, watching everything unfold.

Science class didn't help. The textbooks were outdated, and the explanations for life and reality felt like they were missing the mark entirely. By the time I hit adulthood, that nagging question resurfaced with a vengeance. Determined to find answers, I devoured every book I could on consciousness, the nature of reality, and life's deepest mysteries.

Now, I look at today's world and feel for the younger generation. The adventures of life have been replaced by scrolling through smartphones or living in digital games. Social media has brought some benefits, sure, but it's also served up a cocktail of anxiety, body image issues, and endless comparisons. My hope is that this book reaches those who've lost their sense of wonder and helps them reconnect with the magical, mystical energy that flows through all of us.

Over the past four decades, I have diligently applied my learnings and philosophies, navigating a path marked by both triumphs and challenges. This journey has been deeply influenced by my early aversion to rigid structures; even during my school years, I resisted the confines of being told when and where to spend my day. This intrinsic desire for autonomy naturally led me to pursue self-employment, whether through establishing my own businesses or engaging in freelance work. Embracing such independence is not for the faint-hearted; it demands a steadfast trust in the universe and the courage to let go of conventional securities. However, by attentively aligning one's thoughts and intentions with deliberate actions, the rewards can be profound.

Reflecting on my early years, my first day at school stands out as a vivid illustration of my inherent resistance to imposed structures. Initially I was eager to embark on this new adventure, excited about meeting new friends and discovering what school had to offer. I repeatedly asked, "When is Aunty Christine coming, Mummy?" Christine, though not a blood relative, was a close family friend from two doors down, affectionately called 'Aunty' as was customary then. With several foster children in our home, my mother relied on Christine's support to care for the younger kids while she accompanied me to school. Having not attended any pre-school activities, my anticipation was palpable.

At last, a gentle tap on the front door announced Christine's arrival. In that instant, my excitement evaporated. Panic set in, and I began to bawl and scream as if the world were ending. My mother hurried to put my coat on, with Aunty Christine attempting to help, but my determination to stay home was formidable. They managed to get me as far as the front gate, where I clung with all my might. Gradually, inch by inch, my mother coaxed me up the road toward the alleyway leading to the school. I kicked, screamed, and dug my feet into the pavement, desperate to halt this unfolding nightmare. How could this be happening? Under whose authority was I now required to spend every weekday in a place I hadn't agreed to?

This early defiance against externally imposed schedules foreshadowed my lifelong quest for autonomy. I've consistently sought to live as autonomously as possible, valuing the freedom to determine how I spend my precious time.

Today, I reside in a leafy part of West London with my partner Katie. Amidst the city's bustle, we can still find peace and tranquillity in nature, a testament to the harmony that intentional living can cultivate.

What follows is a culmination of everything I've learned on this lifelong journey. It's for anyone who's ever felt that nagging sense that life is more than just what we see. Together, we'll explore some mind-blowing ideas, question long-held beliefs, and uncover a truth that just might change how you see everything. This book, though concise, is the culmination of over 40 years of learning, reflecting, and living in alignment with these principles. It's my hope that it will inspire you to take control of your own journey and create the life you've always dreamed of.

So, let's dive in and tackle the big question that so often kept me (and maybe you) up at night: *Is consciousness the creator of reality, or just a byproduct of it?*

Introduction: Reality Check—Who's Really in Charge Here?

Modern life is a whirlwind. We wake up, check our phones, rush through the day, and collapse into bed, often without pausing to ask the big questions: *Why am I here? What's the point of all this?* Most of us live life on autopilot, running from one task to the next. But have you ever had a moment—a fleeting, almost magical moment—where everything seemed to stop? Perhaps it was during a beautiful sunset or in the silence of a sleepless night when a tiny voice inside whispered: *Is there more to this than meets the eye?*

That moment isn't just a passing curiosity. It's your inner consciousness tapping you on the shoulder, inviting you to wake up. This book is for anyone who's ever felt that nudge, anyone who suspects that life is far more extraordinary than we've been led to believe.

The undeniable truth is you are not a passive player in life's grand story. You are the author, the director, and the lead actor. Once you understand the principles of consciousness and how reality works, you'll realise you're holding the pen—and you can write any story you desire.

This book is a liberating exploration of the true nature of reality. It will challenge the widely held belief that consciousness is merely a byproduct of the physical world, and instead reveal the astonishing truth: consciousness is the foundation upon which all of existence is built. Armed with this understanding, you will learn to harness the power of your own awareness to shape your life and the world around you.

In this book, we'll explore:

- **The fundamental nature of consciousness** as the creator of reality, uncovering how it shapes everything we perceive and experience.
- **The tools and principles of transformation,** including the power of intention, living in truth, and understanding time as a human construct.
- **The hidden forces of the universe,** diving into quantum physics, parallel realities, and the grand matrix of existence.
- **Practical strategies to elevate your life,** such as harnessing the power of breath, practising gratitude, and mastering the art of surrender.
- **The infinite dimensions of existence,** exploring the dissolution of the ego, the fractal nature of reality, and the illusion of movement in an infinite consciousness.
- **Your ultimate connection to the source,** realising that you are a powerful creator with the ability to shape your reality and fulfil your highest potential.

Table Of Contents

Chapter 1: The Conscious Code

The Big Question

Why does anything exist at all? It's a question that has haunted humanity for millennia. For some, the answer lies in materialism—the idea that the universe is a vast, cold machine, ticking along without meaning or purpose. Consciousness, they argue, is merely a by-product of biological evolution, emerging from random chemical reactions in the brain.

But here's the problem with that view: *Can something ever come from nothing?*

Can Chaos Create Order?

The materialist explanation asks us to believe that, out of a void—complete nothingness—a universe spontaneously erupted. From there, billions of years of blind, chaotic processes somehow led to the intricate beauty and complexity we see today. Every sunset, every snowflake, every Beethoven symphony—all, they say, the result of randomness.

But deep down, we know this doesn't feel right. Chaos doesn't create order. Left to randomness, a pile of bricks doesn't turn into a cathedral, and random scribbles don't become a masterpiece. Even the simplest forms of creation—art, music, poetry—require intention and intelligence.

If we apply this same logic to the universe, we see a different picture: creation is not an accident. It stems from something profound—an underlying source that is eternal, intentional, and infinitely intelligent.

The Source of All: Consciousness

This brings us to the core premise of this book: *Consciousness isn't a by-product of the universe; it is the foundation of reality*. Everything emerges from this field of awareness, which is both omniscient and omnipresent. Let's unpack these terms:

- **Omniscient**: Consciousness contains all knowledge. It's the blueprint of existence, holding every possibility, every solution, every creative spark.
- **Omnipresent**: Consciousness exists everywhere, at all times. It's not confined to your brain or body—it permeates every atom, every particle, every corner of the cosmos.

From this source, the universe arises, not as a random explosion, but as a deliberate expression of infinite potential.

The Observer Effect

Science offers its own fascinating insights into this truth. In quantum physics, particles exist in a state of probability until observed. This is known as the **observer effect**—the act of observation collapses potential outcomes into a single reality.

What does this mean for you? It suggests that your focus, your awareness, plays a crucial role in shaping the reality you experience. You're not just a passive observer; you're an active participant in the creation of your world.

The idea that consciousness shapes reality is vividly demonstrated in quantum mechanics through the "Observer Effect." Scientists have observed that the behaviour of particles, such as electrons, changes depending on whether they are being watched. When observed, these particles act like solid points; when not observed, they behave like waves of potential energy. This suggests that the act of observing—your focus—collapses possibilities into tangible outcomes.

Think of it like this: your attention is like a flashlight in a dark room. Whatever you shine it on becomes illuminated and real in your experience. Without your attention, the room remains filled with countless unseen possibilities. Recognising this, you can begin to see how your focus can shape the unfolding events of your life.

A Universal Puzzle

The nature of consciousness has puzzled humanity for centuries, and different cultures and philosophies offer unique perspectives. Ancient Indian texts describe consciousness as Brahman—the eternal, unchanging reality underlying all existence. In Buddhism, consciousness is seen as both the observer and the experience itself, constantly in flux yet eternal in its presence. Meanwhile, Western science historically viewed consciousness as a byproduct of the brain, though this idea is increasingly challenged by modern discoveries.

These perspectives, while varied, converge on one powerful idea: consciousness is not separate from the universe—it is the universe experiencing itself. By exploring these insights, we open the door to understanding our true nature and the creative power within us.

The Universe Is Inside You

Ancient philosophies, from Advaita Vedanta to Hermeticism, echo a powerful truth: *You are not in the universe; the universe is inside you.* This isn't just a poetic metaphor—it's a literal reflection of how consciousness works.

The core of who you are—your awareness—is connected to the infinite source. Everything you see, hear, and experience is a projection of that source within you.

Consider this: When you dream, entire worlds unfold within your mind. Characters interact, events happen, and yet, it's all taking place within you. In much the same way, your waking life is a projection of the universal consciousness, experienced through your unique lens.

Mind Play: The Nature of Experience

Let's try a little exercise to explore the nature of your reality. Take a moment to recall a vivid dream you've had. Picture it in your mind. Can you remember the scene? Perhaps you were flying through the sky or having a deep conversation with someone who's no longer in your life. Feel the emotions that accompanied that dream—were you excited, scared, or comforted? Notice the colours, the sounds, even the sense of movement. It all felt very real, didn't it?

Now, shift your focus to a memory of a recent summer holiday. Imagine sitting by the ocean, the warmth of the sun on your skin, the gentle crash of waves against the shore. You can almost taste the salty breeze and hear the distant laughter of others enjoying the day. The vivid colours of the sky at sunset, the deep blue of the water, and the golden sand beneath your feet create a tapestry of sensory detail.

Here's the question: Can you truly tell the difference between the dream and the holiday? In both cases, you experienced a rich tapestry of sights, sounds, and emotions. In the moment of recalling them now, they exist as mere memories, yet both seem to share the same mental space. The dream felt incredibly real at the time, and so did the holiday. But now, as you recollect them, they both live as experiences within your consciousness.

This exercise reveals something profound: **reality is a construct of consciousness.** Whether it's the ephemeral landscape of a dream or the seemingly tangible experience of a holiday, both are projections of your awareness. The primary difference lies in the density of the experiences. What you call "reality"—the holiday—is supported by the input of your five senses. It feels more concrete, more "real," because it is reinforced by physical sensations like touch, taste, and smell. Yet, at its core, it is still an experience within consciousness.

In this sense, your consciousness is like a film projector. It creates both the vivid dream and the summer holiday, projecting them onto the screen of your awareness. The dream may be fleeting and intangible, while the holiday feels anchored in the physical world, but both are part of the same creative process.

Consciousness Beyond Physical Life

Given the understanding that consciousness is fundamental, it follows that physical death is not an end but a transition. This perspective is supported by various studies and philosophical arguments suggesting the continuity of consciousness beyond bodily demise. For instance, research into near-death experiences and mediumship provides compelling evidence for the survival of consciousness after death.

Therefore, embracing this view allows us to perceive death not as a final cessation but as a passage to another state of existence. Just as a dream feels vivid and real while you're in it but fades into memory upon waking, so too will the life you've just lived. In your new state of consciousness, everything—your triumphs, challenges, and the rich tapestry of experiences—will seem as ephemeral and dreamlike as your nightly visions do now.

But here's the hopeful part: nothing is ever truly lost. Every experience, every past life, and even the most fleeting of dreams are imprinted in the infinite field of consciousness. Once you reach a higher level of vibration, these memories and insights will be fully accessible to you, enriching your understanding and expanding your awareness. Life, in all its forms, is a perpetual journey of growth, and every chapter remains within your reach.

This isn't a speculative idea but one grounded in extensive research into near-death experiences, past-life regressions, and countless testimonials from individuals who have glimpsed beyond the veil. In your new conscious state, the physical world you once inhabited will feel like a dense, sensory-rich experience you briefly visited, much like the dream you woke from this morning.

The realisation that your consciousness is eternal transforms the fear of death. Life, in this understanding, is not the ultimate reality but rather a temporary projection—an adventure in the infinite field of awareness. And when this chapter of existence ends, your awareness will simply shift, carrying with it the wisdom and growth of this human experience.

Understanding this continuity allows you to view life with a new sense of wonder and detachment. You begin to see that you are not merely living a life; you are exploring a story within the boundless field of consciousness.

The Consciousness Code in Action

Every thought, every emotion, every intention you hold sends ripples through the fabric of reality. The universe isn't something "out there" happening to you; it's a dynamic field responding to your inner state.

When you align your thoughts and emotions with the life you want, you activate the Consciousness Code. You're no longer at the mercy of external circumstances; you become a conscious creator, shaping your reality with precision and purpose.

Conclusion: Unlocking the Code

The idea that consciousness is the foundation of reality is more than a philosophical concept—it's a practical guide to living a life of intention, creativity, and empowerment.

Takeaways from Chapter 1:

Consciousness is not a by-product of the brain but the foundation of all existence. Understanding consciousness empowers you to shape your reality. The "real you" is the awareness that observes and creates, not the fleeting thoughts, emotions or ego personality.

In the next chapter, we'll explore how energy and vibration form the building blocks of this reality, and how aligning with higher frequencies can transform your life.

Chapter 2: The Eternal Dance of Energy

Take a moment to pause and breathe. The air filling your lungs, the beat of your heart, and the hum of the universe around you all share one fundamental truth: *everything is energy.*

From the tiniest particles to the vastness of galaxies, the entire universe vibrates with life. This isn't just an abstract idea; it's a principle rooted in both ancient wisdom and modern science. Understanding this opens the door to deep personal transformation.

The Building Blocks of Reality

Let's start with a simple but mind-blowing fact: at the most fundamental level, everything that appears solid is mostly empty space.

Every atom in your body is 99.9999999999996% empty space, with electrons whizzing around a tiny nucleus at unimaginable speeds. What we perceive as "solid" matter is actually energy fields interacting with each other.

Here's the kicker: when you touch a table, you're not actually touching it. What you feel is the resistance between the negative charge of the electrons in your fingers and those in the table. At a quantum level, there's no physical contact—just energy-repelling energy.

So why does matter feel so real? Because your senses, interpreted by your brain, create the illusion of solidity to help you navigate the world.

Vibration: The Universe's Native Language

Everything in the universe vibrates, from the smallest particle to the largest celestial body. This includes you. Your thoughts, emotions, and even your physical body all emit vibrational frequencies.

The key to understanding how energy shapes your life lies in the principle of resonance. When two objects vibrate at similar frequencies, they resonate and amplify each other. This is why like attracts like. High-frequency emotions such as love, joy, and gratitude resonate with abundance and harmony, while low-frequency emotions like fear, anger, and jealousy attract chaos and negativity.

The Infinite Energy of Empty Space

Let's pause for a moment and consider the concept of empty space. Not just out there amongst the distant stars but the seemingly empty space just in front of you right now. What if I told you that a single cubic metre of so-called "empty" space contains more energy than all the matter in the visible universe?

This isn't science fiction. Physicists have discovered that the vacuum of space is teeming with energy—an almost unfathomable amount known as **zero-point energy**. This energy field, invisible to the naked eye, is the foundation from which all physical matter arises.

Consider This:
Every particle in the universe, every atom in your body, is born from this sea of energy. What appears solid is simply energy vibrating at specific frequencies, temporarily manifesting as matter.

Implication: The universe isn't a cold, lifeless void. It's a dynamic, living field of infinite potential, constantly giving birth to stars, galaxies, trees, flowers and even thoughts.

The Illusion of Solidity

If everything is energy, why does the physical world feel so solid? The answer lies in how our senses interpret these energy fields. Your brain constructs a coherent reality by translating the vibrations around you into sights, sounds, and sensations.

But the solidity you experience is an illusion. At the atomic level, particles are in constant motion, separated by vast stretches of empty space filled with energy.

The Power of Awareness

Understanding that your brain is a filter, not a generator, of consciousness expands your perception of reality. It suggests that your mind has access to the infinite energy field that underpins all existence. This awareness opens the door to tapping into deeper layers of creativity, intuition, and universal wisdom.

Practical Insight: Look Beyond the Illusion

The next time you find yourself in a quiet moment, reflect on the fact that everything you see, touch, and experience is made possible by an invisible ocean of energy. This realisation isn't just a curiosity—it's a key to unlocking the mysteries of existence.

The Power of Vibration in Your Life

Think of your personal vibration as the signal you broadcast to the universe. The energy you emit determines the experiences and opportunities you attract.

If you're operating at a low frequency, focusing on fear or lack, you'll draw in more of the same. Conversely, when you align with high frequencies, you open the door to positive, life-enhancing experiences.

This isn't wishful thinking—it's physics. Just as a tuning fork vibrates in harmony with another of the same frequency, your energy aligns with similar frequencies in the world around you.

You Are Stardust

Here's something extraordinary: every atom in your body was forged in the heart of an ancient star. These atoms have travelled through time and space, forming countless other beings and objects before becoming part of you.

In a very real sense, you are made of stardust, a living testament to the universe's infinite creativity. What's more, your atoms are constantly being recycled, meaning you are physically connected to everything and everyone, past and present.

It's entirely possible that an atom in your body once belonged to a dinosaur, a flower on a distant mountain, or even a historical figure like Jesus or Cleopatra. This cosmic recycling reinforces the idea that life is a continuous, interconnected flow of energy.

Harnessing the Dance of Energy

So how do you tap into this universal dance of energy to transform your life? Here are a few practical steps:

1. **Raise Your Vibration**

Practice gratitude daily. Gratitude is one of the highest vibrational states and has the power to shift your energy instantly.
Engage in acts of kindness. Helping others not only raises their vibration but boosts yours as well.

2. **Align with High-Frequency States**

Focus on love, joy, and abundance. These states naturally attract positive experiences.
Meditate or spend time in nature. Both practices help you tune into the natural rhythms of the universe.

3. **Let Go of Low-Frequency States**

Release anger, resentment, and fear. These emotions act as anchors, keeping you stuck in undesirable realities.

The Science of Energy and Health

Your vibrational state doesn't just affect your mood—it has a direct impact on your physical health. Studies show that practices like meditation, yoga, and mindful breathing can lower stress, reduce inflammation, and improve heart health.

Conclusion: Flow with the Dance

The universe is a symphony of vibrating energy, and you are both an instrument and a composer in this grand orchestra. By raising your vibration and aligning with higher frequencies, you can create a life that resonates with your highest aspirations.

Takeaways from chapter 2:

Energy cannot be created or destroyed; it is the essence of all life and existence. Aligning your personal energy with positive vibrations transforms your life experience. Everything in the universe is connected through an infinite flow of energy.

In the next chapter, we'll explore the role of your brain—not as the creator of consciousness, but as a filter that shapes your human experience.

Chapter 3: The Brain, the Mind, and the Soul Walk Into a Bar

The brain, the mind, and the soul walk into a bar. The bartender, without missing a beat, says, "Let me guess—brain wants a shot of logic, mind needs a strong cocktail of emotions, and soul will have its usual right?"

The brain quips, "Make it a double. I've been solving puzzles all day." The mind groans, "Give me something smooth and calming."
The soul smiles, serene as ever, "just my usual cup of wisdom please."

Three Parts of a Whole

This may not be the funniest joke you've heard, but this playful setup underscores a profound truth: you are not just your brain, mind, or even soul. You are an intricate combination of all three, each playing a unique role in shaping your experience of life. Understanding how they work together—and sometimes against each other—is key to mastering your reality.

The Brain: The Physical Processor

The **brain** is the tangible, physical organ responsible for managing the body's functions and interpreting sensory inputs. It's your biological hardware, an intricate network of neurons firing off electrical signals to keep you alive and alert.

- **Role**: Processes data, manages bodily functions, and reacts to stimuli.

- **Strengths**: Logical thinking, problem-solving, and survival instincts.
- **Limitations**: It's only as good as the data it receives and can be easily overwhelmed.

The Mind: The Intangible Interpreter

The **mind** is where thoughts, emotions, and memories reside. It's the software that interprets the information gathered by the brain, giving meaning to your experiences. Unlike the brain, the mind is intangible—no surgeon could cut you open and point to your thoughts.

- **Role**: Forms beliefs, processes emotions, and drives decision-making.
- **Strengths**: Creative thinking, imagination, and emotional depth.
- **Limitations**: Prone to overthinking, self-doubt, and emotional hijacking.

Example: The brain might register a loud noise, but the mind decides if it's a threat or just the neighbour's dog barking again.

The Soul: The Eternal Observer

The **soul** is your core essence, the timeless and infinite part of you. It exists beyond the physical and mental realms, connecting you to universal consciousness. The soul isn't bound by the limitations of time, space, or logic—it's the quiet observer, always present, always aware.

- **Role**: Provides purpose, intuition, and a sense of connection to something greater.

- **Strengths**: Infinite wisdom, peace, and spiritual guidance.
- **Limitations**: None—it's eternal and unchanging, but it can be drowned out by the noise of the brain and mind.

Perspective: While the brain and mind are busy navigating the complexities of daily life, the soul simply is, waiting for you to tune in and listen.

How They Work Together

1. **Brain**: "I process the data."
2. **Mind**: "I interpret the data."
3. **Soul**: "I provide the meaning beyond the data."

When these three are in harmony, you experience clarity, purpose, and peace. However, when one dominates—like the overactive mind or a stressed-out brain—you can feel disconnected or overwhelmed.

Conflict and Alignment

- **When the Brain Takes Over**:
  The brain, focused on survival and logic, might dismiss intuitive insights as irrational. You might ignore a gut feeling simply because it doesn't "make sense."
- **When the Mind Runs Wild**:
  The mind can spiral into overthinking, creating stories and fears that have no basis in reality. This is where anxiety and self-doubt take root.
- **When the Soul Is Ignored**:
  You may feel unfulfilled, even when everything

seems "right" on paper. The soul's quiet whispers often get lost in the noise of modern life.

Alignment: True balance comes when the brain, mind, and soul operate in harmony—when logic, emotion, and intuition work together to guide your actions.

Practical Exercise: Tuning into the Trio

1. **Quiet the Brain**:
   Find a quiet space and close your eyes. Take a few deep breaths to signal your brain to shift from "problem-solving mode" to a relaxed state.
2. **Calm the Mind**:
   As thoughts arise, acknowledge them without judgement. Imagine them as clouds drifting by—present but not permanent.
3. **Listen to the Soul**:
   Once the brain and mind are quiet, ask yourself: What does my soul want me to know right now? Don't force an answer. Simply remain open and observe what arises.

Conclusion: The Bar Is Always Open

Life is a dance between the brain, the mind, and the soul. Each brings its own unique flavour to the experience, and when they're aligned, they create a symphony of clarity and purpose.

So next time you feel out of sync, remember the bar analogy: your brain may need logic, your mind may crave emotional clarity, and your soul—well, it's always ready for a glass of infinite wisdom on the rocks. Cheers to finding your balance!

Takeaways from Chapter 3:

The brain processes information, the mind interprets it, and the soul connects you to infinite awareness. Together, these components create your perception of reality. Harmony between these elements leads to greater self-awareness and clarity.

Chapter 4: The Brain—Not Your Average Tour Guide

If you've ever thought of your brain as the all-powerful control centre of your life, you're about to be pleasantly surprised. While the brain is extraordinary, it's not the master of reality—it's a tool, a filter, and, most importantly, a guide.

The Brain as a Filter, Not a Creator

The common belief is that your brain *creates* consciousness, but this is a misinterpretation. Instead, the brain acts as a filter, tuning into the vast field of consciousness and limiting your experience so you can navigate the world in a manageable way.

Think of consciousness as the internet—limitless, all-encompassing, and always available. Your brain is like a web browser. It doesn't *generate* the internet; it simply connects to a specific part of it, delivering the information you need in that moment.

The Science of Changing Beliefs

One of the brain's most remarkable abilities is its capacity for neuroplasticity—the ability to rewire itself by forming new neural connections, known as synapses. This process is activated when we repeatedly think about or focus on new beliefs and ideas. Each time you introduce a new concept to your mind and consciously reinforce it, your brain physically changes to support this new way of thinking.

For example, studies show that when people practice gratitude daily, their brain rewires itself to notice positive aspects of their lives more easily. Similarly, visualising a goal repeatedly creates neural pathways that help align your thoughts and actions to achieve that goal.

This physical transformation in the brain is proof that changing your thoughts isn't just a mental exercise—it's a biological one. It's as if the brain is a gardener, pruning away unused pathways and nurturing new ones based on the seeds of thought you choose to plant and water.

The Radio Analogy

A more relatable metaphor: your brain is like a radio. When you turn on the radio, it tunes into a specific frequency and plays music. But the music doesn't originate in the radio—it's coming from a broader network of signals.

Similarly, consciousness exists independently of the brain. Your brain tunes into the "station" that allows you to experience life as a human being. Looking for consciousness inside the brain is like searching for musicians inside the radio.

If the brain truly generates consciousness, why is our perception of reality so limited? We only see a narrow band of the electromagnetic spectrum (visible light), hear a restricted range of sound frequencies, and rely on a few basic senses to interpret the world. This raises a fascinating question: if reality is infinite and all-encompassing, why do we perceive only a tiny sliver of it?

The answer lies in the brain's role as a **filter**. Rather than showing us everything, it carefully curates our experience, narrowing down the overwhelming flood of information into something manageable. This selective filtering allows us to function effectively as human beings, focusing on the immediate tasks and challenges of life.

But what if the brain's filter were lifted? What if we could suddenly perceive the full spectrum of reality—the countless dimensions, energies, and frequencies that surround us? It's likely that such an experience would be so vast, so incomprehensibly rich, that it would quite literally *blow our minds*. The brain's limitations are not flaws; they're survival mechanisms, allowing us to navigate the physical world without being consumed by its infinite complexity.

What Happens When the Filter Shifts?

When the brain's filter loosens—through near-death experiences, meditation, or psychedelics—people often report expanded states of awareness:

- **Near-Death Experiences (NDEs)**: People in these states frequently describe heightened awareness, profound peace, and even encounters with otherworldly realms. Remarkably, many NDEs occur when brain activity is minimal or absent, suggesting consciousness exists beyond the physical brain.
- **Psychedelics**: Substances like 5-MeO-DMT can temporarily dissolve the ego and reveal a boundless, interconnected reality. Users often describe seeing intricate fractals and feeling one with the universe, supporting the idea that the

brain typically filters out much of what's "really out there."

Your Ego: The Narrator of Your Story

The brain houses the **Default Mode Network (DMN)**, a system responsible for self-referential thinking. This is where your ego lives—the part of you that constructs your personal identity and narrates your life story.

While the ego helps you navigate daily life, it can also be limiting. It thrives on control, fear, and comparison, often pulling you away from your true, infinite nature.

By quieting the DMN—through meditation or other practices—you can silence the ego and connect with a deeper, more expansive awareness.

How Your Brain Shapes Your Reality

Your brain's filter doesn't just limit what you perceive; it also colours your experience based on your beliefs, memories, and expectations.

- If you believe the world is full of danger, your brain will filter for threats, highlighting every negative news story or unsettling encounter.
- If you believe the world is abundant and full of opportunity, your brain will filter for positive experiences, drawing your attention to opportunities and uplifting connections.

This is why it's so important to master your inner dialogue. Your thoughts literally shape the way your brain filters reality. Try this: choose a belief or idea you'd like to strengthen in your life. It could be something like, "I am capable of achieving my dreams," or, "I live a life full of abundance." Each day, spend a few moments visualising this belief as if it were already true. Speak it aloud with confidence, and imagine what your life would look like if this belief guided your actions.

Over time, this simple exercise reinforces the neural pathways associated with this belief, making it easier for your brain to adopt it as part of your reality.

Practical Tips for Reprogramming Your Filter

1. **Meditate Regularly**
   Meditation helps quiet the noise of the ego and DMN, allowing you to connect with the vast consciousness beyond your brain's filter.
2. **Set Positive Intentions**
   Begin each day by affirming your desired reality. This primes your brain to filter for experiences that align with your goals.
3. **Challenge Negative Beliefs**
   When negative thoughts arise, ask yourself: *Is this absolutely true?* By questioning these beliefs, you weaken their influence on your brain's filtering system.
4. **Gratitude Journaling**
   Spend a few minutes each day writing down things you're grateful for. Gratitude shifts your focus to abundance, helping your brain filter for positive experiences.

The Soul's Role in the Equation

Amid the dynamic interplay between the brain and mind lies the soul—the unchanging essence of who you truly are. Unlike the brain and mind, which are constantly evolving and adapting, the soul remains a silent observer, providing a sense of continuity and purpose. It is your soul that nudges you toward alignment with higher truths and guides you in recognising when a belief or thought resonates deeply.

While the brain and mind manage the mechanics of life, the soul offers a compass, helping you navigate with clarity and authenticity. Together, these three aspects of your being create the unique, multi-dimensional experience of what it means to be human

Conclusion: Trust the Guide, But Know the Source

Your brain is an extraordinary tool, helping you navigate the human experience. But remember, it's not the source of your consciousness—it's simply a guide. By understanding its role, you can break free from its limitations and connect with the infinite awareness that is your true self.

Takeaways from Chapter 4:

The brain is a filter for consciousness, not its creator. It limits our experience to what's necessary for human life, shielding us from overwhelming information. Expanding awareness allows you to transcend the brain's filters and perceive more of reality.

In the next chapter, we'll dive into the Multiverse Café, exploring the limitless possibilities of parallel realities and how your choices shape the life you experience.

Chapter 5: Welcome to the Multiverse Café

Imagine walking into a vibrant café where every table represents a different version of your life. At one table, you're an acclaimed author. At another, you're a world traveller, or perhaps a scientist who's just made a groundbreaking discovery. In this café, every possible version of your life exists simultaneously, waiting for you to choose which table to sit at. Welcome to the Multiverse Café.

Parallel Realities: More Than Science Fiction

The concept of the multiverse, once relegated to science fiction, is now gaining traction in scientific and philosophical circles. Quantum physics, in particular, suggests that multiple realities coexist, branching out with every decision you make.

Consider this: each choice you make—no matter how small—splits reality into new possibilities. Didn't take that job? There's a version of you that did. Decided to move to a new city? Somewhere, another version of you stayed put.

These alternate realities are not mere fantasies. They're potential versions of your life that exist in parallel, shaped by your intentions and actions.

The Observer Effect and the Role of Choice

Quantum mechanics introduces a fascinating phenomenon known as the **observer effect**. Until observed, particles exist in a state of probability, embodying all possible outcomes simultaneously. But the moment they are observed, they "collapse" into a single, specific state.

In much the same way, your focus and choices collapse the infinite possibilities of the multiverse into the reality you experience. You are both the observer and the creator, shaping your path with every decision and intention.

Your Choices Are Powerful

Every decision you make, no matter how small, is like ordering from the menu at the Multiverse Café. Whether you choose to take a new job, start a business, or focus on personal growth, your choices set the trajectory for your life.

But here's the liberating truth: you can always make new choices. If you don't like the table you're currently seated at, you can get up and choose another. The multiverse offers infinite do-overs.

Manifesting in the Multiverse

The multiverse doesn't just passively exist—it responds to your intentions. When you set a clear goal and align your thoughts, emotions, and actions with that goal, you effectively signal the universe to shift you toward a reality where your desire already exists.

Exercise: Your Multiverse Order

- Imagine you're at the Multiverse Café. What reality would you like to order?
- Write down your "order" in a journal, stating it as if it's already happening: *I am living a joyful, abundant life.*

- Reflect on the steps you can take to align your current actions with that desired reality.

Patience and the Art of Timing

One of the hardest parts of manifesting is trusting the process. Just as you wouldn't demand your meal the moment you place an order, you need to give the universe time to align the pieces. Trust that everything is unfolding as it should, even if you don't see immediate results.

Sometimes, what appears to be a delay is actually a redirection, guiding you to an even better outcome.

Recognising Signs and Synchronicities

The universe often communicates through subtle signs and synchronicities. Pay attention to those moments of uncanny coincidence—a chance meeting, a song lyric that speaks to you, or an unexpected opportunity. These are the universe's way of nudging you toward your desired reality.

The Butterfly Effect in Your Life

In chaos theory, the butterfly effect suggests that a small action, like the flap of a butterfly's wings, can set off a chain of events leading to significant outcomes. In your life, minor decisions—choosing to say yes to an invitation, taking a different route home—can lead to profound changes. Perhaps you've experienced this in your own life. Maybe you took a last-minute trip and met someone who became a lifelong friend or mentor. Reflect on these moments and consider how they've shaped your path.

Conclusion: Take Your Seat at the Café

The Multiverse Café is open, and the possibilities are endless. Your choices and intentions determine which reality you experience, so choose wisely. By understanding the power of your focus and decisions, you can consciously navigate the multiverse to create a life that excites and fulfils you.

Takeaways from Chapter 5:

Every decision you make opens a pathway to a new reality. The multiverse contains infinite possibilities shaped by your choices and intentions. You have the power to step into the version of reality you most desire.

Chapter 6: The Morning I Defied Gravity

June 1, 1986, began like any other day in Bournemouth, but it was destined to become a pivotal chapter in my journey toward understanding consciousness. The night before, a Saturday, my friend Craig and I had ventured into our usual haunt—a bustling nightclub where the music thumped, and the crowd swayed in unison to the sound of "The Sun Always Shines on TV" by A-ha. Seeking a brief respite from the chaos, we retreated to a quieter sidebar.

In the mid-1980s, our social circle was defined by a distinctive gothic aesthetic. The girls often donned black attire, heavy eyeliner, and backcombed hair, exuding a mysterious allure. The air was frequently thick with the earthy scent of patchouli oil, a hallmark of the era's alternative fashion.

Amidst this sea of dark rebellion, Johanna stood out with her elegant style and exceptional talent as a trained dancer. Her movements on the dance floor were captivating, drawing attention and admiration. I'd noticed her for months, always accompanied by her overprotective boyfriend. Interestingly, he had often gossiped about me and my friends, painting a picture that, unbeknownst to him, piqued Johanna's curiosity about me. That night, however, she was celebrating her 18th birthday with just her twin brother, who had wandered elsewhere in the venue. Seizing the opportunity, I introduced myself.

"I know who you are," she replied with a tipsy smile. Her boyfriend's tales had sparked an intrigue, making her more receptive to our conversation. Rumours had cast me as a privileged 'rich kid' musician with an impressive recording studio. In reality, I came from humble beginnings, manifesting my studio through intention and action. But I wasn't about to dispel the myths that night. We exchanged numbers, and I promised to call.

Craig and I crashed at my parents' house, tasked with keeping an eye on the place during their absence. Around 6:30 a.m., I awoke rather parched from the previous night's revelry. Too relaxed to fetch water, I lay still, noticing a tiny, dancing light piercing through the curtains. The light moved gracefully, performing an intricate ballet across the room. It would descend toward my head, almost as if inspecting me, then retreat back to the window, only to repeat the mesmerising dance. At this stage, I watched in bemusement, not yet feeling any fear.

Simultaneously, a tingling sensation spread across the back of my head. Amused, I chuckled at the whimsical light.

Deciding to rise, I swung my legs over the bed, only to find them growing inexplicably heavy. By the time I reached the door, I was paralysed from the waist down—I was terrified and also fascinated by what I was experiencing. Looking up, I saw a matrix of bluish-white lines of electricity streaming from the window across the ceiling. Attempting to speak the word 'electricity' in amazement, my voice emerged deep and resonant, with an echo that lingered endlessly.

Suddenly, but gently, I was lifted horizontally, levitated in mid-air, drifting ever so slowly back toward my bed. I tried to call out to Craig, but my voice faltered. As I hovered above the bed, I felt myself gently lowered back into my body, regaining control and bolting upright, trembling with fear.

Mustering the strength to stand, the head vibrations returned, and I was momentarily separated from my body again before being pulled or pushed back in. Cautiously, I managed to make my way downstairs for that much-needed water. At the time, I had no explanation for the terrifying experience. But it reignited my quest to understand consciousness, affirming that my awareness, or consciousness, thrived even when seemingly detached from my physical form.

Determined to comprehend these phenomena, I immersed myself in literature on the subject. However, in the mid-1980s, resources on out-of-body experiences (OBEs) were scarce. One notable work was Robert A. Monroe's "Far Journeys," published in 1985, which delved into his explorations beyond the physical realm. Through dedicated meditation practice, I occasionally managed to induce OBEs on demand. However, each journey was accompanied by fear, snapping me back into my body prematurely.

One night, while attempting to leave my body, I heard two men conversing. Panicked, I opened my eyes but saw no one. Realising these voices were coming from within, I mentally questioned their presence. Incredibly, they responded with, "Oh, you can hear us." Amazed, I affirmed, and they advised me to gently rock from side to side to facilitate the process rather than trying to sit bolt upright, which was my normal method. I never heard them again, but their guidance proved effective.

Despite these experiences, I never grew accustomed to the sensation of leaving my body. Eventually, I ceased these practices as everyday life concerns took over.

And yes, I did call Johanna later the following week. Our connection blossomed, leading to the birth of our beautiful daughter, Helena—a radiant light and the greatest gift of my life.

This encounter was a catalyst, propelling me deeper into the mysteries of consciousness and the boundless potential of the human spirit.

In the next chapter, we'll delve into the practical power of intention, exploring how your thoughts and beliefs act as the blueprint for your reality.

Chapter 7: The Power of Intention

Intent is a small word with enormous implications. It's the invisible force behind every decision, every action, and every outcome in your life. Whether you're aware of it or not, your intentions are shaping your reality every moment of every day.

But here's the twist: by learning to harness the power of intention deliberately, you can transform your life in ways you never thought possible.

Intention: The Blueprint of Reality

Intention is not a vague hope or wish—it's a clear, focused declaration of what you will create. It aligns your thoughts, emotions, and actions with your desired outcome, sending a powerful signal to the universe.

The universe operates like a mirror, reflecting back the energy you project. If your intention is rooted in fear or lack, that's what you'll see mirrored in your life. But when your intention is clear and aligned with love, abundance, and growth, the universe responds in kind.

The Science of Intention

Studies have shown that focused intention can influence outcomes, even at a distance. In one famous experiment conducted by the Princeton Engineering Anomalies Research (PEAR) lab, participants were able to affect the behaviour of random number generators simply by focusing their thoughts.

Another compelling example comes from Dr. Masaru Emoto's water experiments. By directing positive words or intentions toward water, Emoto demonstrated that water crystals formed beautiful, harmonious patterns. Negative intentions, on the other hand, produced chaotic, distorted patterns.

These experiments suggest that intention has the power to influence not just our personal reality but the physical world around us.

Intention as a Moral Compass

Intention doesn't just shape outcomes; it also serves as a guide for ethical decision-making and a moral compass. Consider the question: *Is it ever okay to physically harm someone or even kill?* On the surface, the answer seems obvious—no. But what if you were in a situation where using extreme force, therefore harming or even killing someone, was the only way to protect the innocent life of a child?

Here, your intention matters. If your action is driven by the intention to protect and save, then it aligns with higher principles, even if the outcome is not ideal. Understanding this can help you reconcile past actions where you may have done wrong, knowing your intent was honourable.

Choosing Between Fear and Love: A Reflection Exercise

Life presents us with two guiding forces: **Love** and **Fear**. These two energies influence our thoughts, actions, and relationships, shaping the reality we experience. To gain clarity on which force is driving your decisions, let's engage in a simple but profound exercise.

Love vs. Fear: Let Battle Commence

Take a notebook and open it to a blank double-page spread. On the **left-hand page**, write the word **Fear** at the top in bold letters. On the **right-hand page**, write **Love**.

Now, let's examine these two guiding forces more closely.

Fear's Heavy Load

Fear can manifest in many forms—anger, jealousy, blame or hatred. It's a reactive state that pulls us away from our true potential and connection to others. Under the Fear heading, list every fear-based emotion or behaviour you can think of. Here are a few to get started:

- Hatred (the cornerstone)
- Anger
- Resentment
- Envy
- Selfishness
- Blame
- Doubt
- Shame

Fear thrives on control, separation, and resistance, dragging us into a state of limitation and conflict.

The Light of Love

Now, shift your focus to the right-hand page. Love is the highest vibration, a unifying force that fosters connection, healing, and growth. The number one virtue of Love is **forgiveness**. Forgiveness is the antidote to the poison of fear—it releases the past, liberates your heart, and clears the way for healing and peace.

Under the Love heading, write down all the virtues and emotions that embody this energy:

- Forgiveness (the cornerstone)
- Compassion
- Gratitude
- Honesty
- Kindness
- Patience
- Joy
- Empathy
- Generosity

The more you come from the Love page, the more aligned you become with your highest self and the infinite source of energy around you.

Using This Exercise as a Guide

Whenever you face a challenge or a decision, revisit this exercise. Ask yourself: Am I acting from the Fear page or the Love page? If your words or actions stem from fear, take a moment to realign. Focus on forgiveness, understanding, or gratitude.

Reflection

This practice will help you navigate conflicts, especially in relationships. If you've had an argument with a friend or partner, consider which side of the notebook you were operating from. Be honest with yourself. Were your words driven by anger or fear of losing control, or did they stem from a place of compassion and patience?

If the outcome wasn't what you desired, but your intention was rooted in love, be kind to yourself. Coming from Love doesn't always guarantee the desired external results, but it always elevates your internal state and keeps you aligned with your higher purpose.

Choosing Love Daily

Every day, you're given the choice to live from Fear or Love. By practising this exercise, you'll not only gain insight into your emotional patterns but also cultivate a habit of leaning into love's virtues. Over time, you'll find that the Love page grows fuller, while the Fear page fades into the background.

The Power Lies Within You

Remember this: in life, it's not important what others do, say, or think. The only thing that truly matters is how you choose to act, speak, and respond. Your behaviour, intentions, and actions are the threads that weave the fabric of your life. It's easy to get caught up in the words and actions of others, allowing their behaviour to dictate your emotional state or self-worth. But the truth is, you have no control over others. They act according to their own perspectives, experiences, and fears. Trying to control or change them is not only futile but also distracts you from the one thing you can control: yourself.

Be the Lighthouse

In a world often clouded by fear, doubt, and negativity, choose to be the lighthouse. Lighthouses do not chase ships; they simply stand tall, shining their light, guiding others home. Similarly, your steady presence, grounded in love and integrity, will inspire and uplift those around you, even without words.

In the end, it's not what happens around you that defines your life—it's how you navigate the waves. You are the captain of your ship, the creator of your experience, and the source of your peace.

The Freedom of Self-Mastery

When you realise that your peace and happiness are not tied to anyone else's actions, you step into a powerful place of freedom. Your energy is no longer wasted on reactions, blame, or resentment. Instead, it is channelled into creating a life aligned with your highest values.

Ask yourself in every situation:

- Am I acting with integrity?
- Am I coming from love, or am I operating from fear?
- Does my behaviour reflect the person I aspire to be?

Your Behaviour Shapes Your World

Your actions ripple outward, influencing the world in ways you may never fully see or understand. When you choose kindness in the face of cruelty, patience in the face of frustration, or forgiveness in the face of hurt, you elevate not only your own vibration but also the collective energy around you.

It's not about seeking validation or approval from others. It's about knowing, deep within, that you are living authentically and honourably.

Aligning Intentions with Action

Intentions alone are not enough; they must be paired with inspired action. When your thoughts, emotions, and actions are in harmony, you create a powerful current that propels you toward your goals.

Practical Exercise: Affirming Intentions

Health
I am connected to the source of vibrant energy and vitality. My body heals, renews, and strengthens itself naturally. I radiate health and well-being in every moment.

Relationships
I am connected to the universal field of love and attract meaningful, nurturing relationships. I give and receive love freely, and my connections bring joy, growth, and harmony.

Creativity
I am connected to the boundless source of inspiration and creativity. Ideas flow to me effortlessly, and I bring them to life with confidence and passion.

Wealth
I am connected to the infinite source of abundance and effortlessly attract financial prosperity into my life. Money flows to me easily, and I use it to create joy and freedom.

General Affirmation
I am aligned with the source of all that exists, and everything I desire flows to me at the right time and in the right way.

- Repeat these affirmations daily, visualising your desired outcome as if it has already happened.

By affirming your intentions as a present reality, you align yourself with the energy of that reality, making it easier to manifest.

Patience: The Silent Ally of Intention

One of the most challenging aspects of working with intention is trusting the process. The universe doesn't operate on human timelines. Sometimes, the seeds of intention take time to grow, and patience is required to see them come to fruition.

Anecdote:
Years ago, while working a low-paid temporary job at the Earl's Court Motor Show, I found myself mesmerised by a stunning British racing green BMW convertible, slowly rotating on an electric platform. I wasn't in a position to buy it at the time, but something inside me quietly declared, *One day, I'll have a car like this.*

Fast forward five years: out of the blue, a colleague mentioned he was selling his BMW. When I went to take a look, there it was—the exact same shade of British racing green. In that moment, I realised the universe had been working behind the scenes, aligning circumstances perfectly with my original intention. The desire I had set in motion years earlier had finally come full circle. Without hesitation, I bought the car.

This experience was a powerful reminder: the universe never forgets. Even when our conscious mind moves on, the seeds we plant through our intentions continue to grow, waiting for the right moment to blossom.

Recognising Resistance

Sometimes, intentions don't manifest as expected. This is often due to internal resistance—subconscious beliefs or fears that conflict with your desires.

Ask yourself:

- Do I truly believe I deserve this?
- Am I holding onto fear or doubt that's blocking my progress?

Once you identify and release these blocks, your intentions can flow more freely.

Living Intentionally Every Day

Intention isn't just for big life goals; it's a tool you can use in everyday life. Start your day by setting an intention, whether it's to approach your tasks with focus, to connect deeply with others, or simply to find joy in small moments.

By living intentionally, you create a life that aligns with your highest values and aspirations.

Conclusion: Mastering the Power of Intention

Intention is your most powerful tool for creating the life you desire. When you align your thoughts, emotions, and actions with clear, purposeful intentions, you become a co-creator with the universe.

Takeaways from Chapter 7:

Intention is the blueprint for manifesting your reality. Focus on what you desire, not on what you fear or lack. Use positive affirmations like "I am" or "I will" to set clear, actionable goals.

Chapter 8: Let Truth be Your Lighthouse: Navigating Life's Waters

Truth Is; Everything Else Is Deception

Truth stands immutable. It is not subject to interpretation, distortion, or the passage of time. Anything that veers from truth—no matter how slight—carries a degree of deception. This deception, whether a small omission or a grand falsehood, generates varying levels of destructive energy, distorting our reality and disconnecting us from our higher selves.

Why is truth so powerful? Because it aligns perfectly with the universal fabric of existence. Truth vibrates at the highest frequency, cutting through the noise of illusion and falsehood. It is the only foundation upon which a truly fulfilling and harmonious life can be built.

"The Truth Will Set You Free"

When Jesus said, "The truth will set you free," he spoke to the liberating power of aligning with truth. Living in truth dissolves the chains of fear, guilt, and shame—the emotions that bind us when we live in deception. Truth liberates the mind, offering clarity and peace where confusion and inner conflict once reigned.

1. **Freedom from Illusion**:
   Deceptions, even self-deceptions, create a false reality. This false reality might feel safe or convenient in the short term, but it leads to inner turmoil. Truth dispels illusions, providing a clear, unshakeable foundation for life.

2. **Freedom from Fear**:
   Fear thrives in the shadow of deception. When you live in truth, you no longer need to fear exposure or judgement. You stand in the light, confident and unburdened.
3. **Freedom to Create**:
   Truth aligns you with the creative power of the universe. When you operate from a place of truth, your intentions and actions carry a purity that accelerates manifestation and attracts abundance.

The Destructive Energy of Deception

Deception doesn't just distort your external world; it wreaks havoc on your internal state. Every time you lie—to yourself or others—you introduce a conflict between your actions and your higher self. This conflict manifests as anxiety, stress, and even physical ailments over time.

- **Self-Deception**: The most insidious form. Convincing yourself that something is fine when it's not, or ignoring the quiet voice of your intuition, pulls you further from your true path.
- **Lies to Others**: They create barriers in relationships, erode trust, and foster environments of fear and control.

Even the smallest lie introduces disharmony, like a pebble creating ripples in a still pond. The more significant the deception, the more destructive the ripples become, often leading to larger crises or breakdowns.

Truth as the Highest Energy

Truth doesn't just "exist" in a passive sense; it actively shapes reality. It aligns with the natural order of the universe, reinforcing harmony and balance. Living in truth raises your vibration, enhancing your physical, emotional, and spiritual well-being.

Examples of Truth's High Energy:

- Relationships based on honesty flourish in trust and mutual respect.
- Business ventures guided by integrity attract loyal clients and sustainable success.
- Personal growth accelerates when you face your truths, even the hard ones.

Why Living in Truth Is Essential for Creation

When you live in truth, you align your thoughts, words, and actions with the universal energy that creates worlds. Any deception, however small, introduces resistance into this process.

Consider truth as a straight, unbroken line connecting you to your goals. Lies and self-deceptions create detours, delays, and obstacles. When your life is rooted in truth, your path to manifestation becomes clear and direct.

Facing Hard Truths: The Courage to Align

Living in truth requires courage. It means facing the parts of your life where you've strayed, acknowledging mistakes, and choosing to realign. While this process can be uncomfortable, it is profoundly freeing and transformative.

- **Reflection**: Ask yourself, Where am I not living in full alignment with truth?
- **Forgiveness**: Truth may reveal areas where forgiveness is needed—whether of yourself or others. Embrace this as part of the healing journey.

Practical Steps to Live in Truth

1. **Daily Truth Check**: Before making decisions or speaking, pause and ask: Is this true? Is this in alignment with who I am?
2. **Honest Communication**: Practice truth in your interactions. Speak your truth with kindness and clarity, even when it's difficult.
3. **Self-Reflection**: Regularly journal or meditate to explore areas of your life where you may be avoiding or distorting truth.
4. **Trust Your Intuition**: Often, your intuition nudges you toward truth. Learn to trust that inner voice.

The Ripple Effect of Truth

Living in truth doesn't just transform your life; it influences the world around you. Truth inspires trust, strengthens relationships, and creates environments of authenticity and respect. Your commitment to truth sets a powerful example, encouraging others to do the same.

Conclusion: Truth as Your North Star

Truth isn't just a guiding principle; it's the foundation of a life well-lived. It liberates, empowers, and aligns you with the creative force of the universe. By committing to truth, you not only free yourself from the destructive energy of deception but also pave the way for a life of clarity, peace, and fulfilment.

In the end, truth is not just what sets you free—it's what sets you apart.

Takeaways from Chapter 8:

Truth is the most powerful guiding principle for creating a fulfilling life. Living authentically aligns you with higher vibrations and liberates you from deception. Honesty with yourself and others creates a foundation for growth and meaningful relationships.

Chapter 9: Life Is a Soap Opera, and You're the Screen

Life often feels like a chaotic drama—a never-ending series of events, emotions, and challenges. We play different roles: the hero, the victim, the friend, the lover, the fighter. The plot twists can be thrilling, heartbreaking, or downright absurd.

But what if you're not just the character in this story? What if you're something much more profound—the silent, unchanging presence that watches the drama unfold?

The Screen and the Movie

Rupert Spira, a contemporary teacher of non-duality, offers a brilliant metaphor to explain this concept. He likens consciousness to a TV screen and the events of life to a movie playing on it. The movie may contain moments of joy, sorrow, love, and loss, but the screen itself remains unchanged.

No matter how intense the drama or how vivid the scenes, the screen is never affected. It doesn't become wet in a rainstorm or burned in a fire. Similarly, your true self—your awareness—is untouched by the ups and downs of life.

Why This Matters

When you identify solely with the character in the story, life can feel overwhelming. Every setback, every heartbreak feels personal and defining. But when you realise that you are the screen—the unchanging, ever-present awareness—you gain a real and deep sense of peace.

You can watch the drama unfold without being consumed by it. You can experience emotions without being controlled by them.

Becoming the Observer

To truly embrace this perspective, you must learn to observe your thoughts and emotions without judgement. This doesn't mean suppressing or ignoring them. Instead, it's about recognising that they are temporary experiences passing through your awareness.

Exercise: Practising Awareness

- Find a quiet place to sit and close your eyes.
- Imagine yourself as a screen, and let the "movie" of your thoughts and feelings play out.
- Observe without getting caught up in the story. Simply notice the thoughts and emotions as they come and go.

With practice, you'll begin to see that your true self—the observer—is separate from the drama.

Real-Life Application

Let's say you're in the middle of an argument with someone you care about. In the heat of the moment, it's easy to feel consumed by anger or frustration. But if you pause and remember that you are the screen, not the scene, you can step back and respond from a place of calm and clarity.

This doesn't mean you won't feel emotions. You will. But you'll no longer be a slave to them. Instead, you'll be able to navigate life's challenges with grace and perspective.

Why the Drama Is Necessary

Here's an interesting twist: while the drama of life can be exhausting, it's also essential for growth. Just as a movie needs conflict to drive the plot, your life's challenges push you to learn, evolve, and expand.

The key is to engage with life fully while remembering that your true essence—the screen—is always at peace.

Conclusion: Embrace Your Dual Role

You are both the actor in life's drama and the screen on which it unfolds. By embracing this dual role, you can experience life's richness without losing yourself in its intensity.

Takeaways from Chapter 9:

You are not the drama of your life; you are the observer behind it all. Detach from emotional reactions and see life's events as part of a larger story. Stay grounded in the awareness that you are the unchanging presence behind life's ups and downs.

In the next chapter, we'll explore how quantum physics and consciousness intersect, revealing the mystical ways in which your awareness shapes reality.

Chapter 10: Consciousness Meets Quantum Weirdness

Quantum physics is a world where the rules we know—solid, predictable, logical—start to dissolve. In this realm, particles can exist in two places at once, decisions seem to create reality, and observation itself becomes a powerful force. It's a playground of possibilities, and at the heart of it all lies consciousness.

But what does this have to do with you? Quite a lot, actually. Welcome to the intersection of quantum mechanics and the mind—a place where science meets the profound truths of existence.

The Double-Slit Experiment: Reality Responds to You

One of the most famous experiments in quantum physics is the **double-slit experiment**. When particles (like electrons) are fired at a barrier with two slits, they behave like waves, creating an interference pattern on the other side.

But here's the twist: when scientists observe the particles, they stop behaving like waves and start acting like particles, passing through one slit or the other. Simply put, the act of observation changes the outcome.

This baffling result suggests that reality isn't fixed. It responds to the observer. In a very real sense, the universe waits for your input to decide how it will behave.

Schrödinger's Cat: The Power of Potential

Imagine a cat in a box. Alongside it is a vial of poison, triggered by the decay of a radioactive particle. According to quantum mechanics, until you open the box and observe, the cat is both alive and dead—a superposition of states.

This thought experiment, known as **Schrödinger's Cat**, highlights a crucial concept: reality exists as potential until it's observed.

In your life, countless potential realities exist simultaneously. The version of you who takes a new job, moves to a different country, or starts a creative project—all these possibilities coexist. It's your focus and choices that "open the box" and bring a specific reality into being.

The Role of Consciousness

If particles behave differently when observed, what does that say about consciousness? It suggests that consciousness isn't just a passive observer; it's an active participant in shaping reality.

This aligns perfectly with the concept of the **observer effect** in your daily life. Your thoughts, intentions, and beliefs influence the reality you experience. You're not just a spectator in the universe; you're a co-creator.

Quantum Entanglement: We're All Connected

Another mind-bending phenomenon in quantum physics is **entanglement**. When two particles become entangled, their states are linked, no matter how far apart they are.

Change the state of one particle, and the other instantly changes as well.

This isn't just a quirky feature of the quantum world—it speaks to a deeper truth about the interconnectedness of everything. At a fundamental level, you are connected to every person, place, and thing in the universe.

This could explain the sense of oneness people often feel during intense spiritual experiences or even why you might think of a friend just moments before they call.

Living in a Quantum Reality

How can you apply these quantum insights to your daily life? Here are a few key takeaways:

1. **Your Focus Shapes Reality**
   Just as particles behave differently under observation, your life aligns with what you focus on. Are you focusing on problems or possibilities? Lack or abundance? Shift your focus, and watch your reality transform.
2. **Embrace Uncertainty**
   In the quantum world, uncertainty is a feature, not a bug. Embrace the unknown as a space of infinite potential. It's where all possibilities exist, waiting for you to choose and act.
3. **Recognise Your Connections**
   Remember that you're not isolated. Your thoughts, actions, and energy ripple out, influencing the collective reality. Use this knowledge to cultivate compassion, empathy, and positive intentions.

Mind-Bending Fact: Everything Happens at Once

Here's a thought that will blow your mind: in the quantum realm, time as we know it doesn't exist. Past, present, and future coexist in a single, eternal now.

This suggests that every possibility is already out there, waiting for you to step into it. You don't have to "create" your ideal life from scratch—it already exists. Your role is to align with it and bring it into your experience.

Conclusion: Embrace the Quantum Mindset

Quantum physics reveals a universe far more flexible, dynamic, and participatory than we ever imagined. By understanding the role of consciousness in shaping reality, you can step into your power as a co-creator.

Takeaways from Chapter 10:

Quantum physics reveals that observation shapes reality. Your awareness plays a direct role in creating outcomes. Embrace uncertainty as a space of potential and creation.

In the next chapter, we'll explore the concept of infinity, diving into the boundless nature of existence and what it means for your life.

Chapter 11: Infinity—The Boundless Nature of Reality

Take a moment to imagine the infinite. It's not easy, is it? The human mind is accustomed to boundaries—beginnings and endings, limits and edges. Yet, the universe defies these constraints. It stretches endlessly in all directions, both outward into the cosmos and inward into the tiniest particles of existence.

Infinity is more than a mind-boggling concept; it's a fundamental truth of reality. And what's even more astonishing? You are an intrinsic part of it.

Fractals: Infinity Within the Finite

One of the most beautiful illustrations of infinity can be found in fractals. These are complex patterns that repeat infinitely at every scale. No matter how much you zoom in or out, the pattern remains consistent, revealing endless layers of detail.

The universe itself behaves like a fractal. From the swirling galaxies to the branching veins of a leaf, the same patterns and principles repeat across different scales. This isn't just poetic; it's mathematical.

When people experience ego dissolution during deep meditation or on substances like **5-MeO-DMT**, many report visions of intricate fractals, as if they're peering into the very fabric of reality. These fractals symbolise the infinite, interconnected nature of existence.

You Are the Universe, and the Universe Is You

Ancient philosophies and spiritual teachings have long suggested that *you are not in the universe; the universe is in you.* This isn't just a metaphor—it's a profound truth.

If consciousness is the foundation of reality, then everything you experience, every star you gaze at, and every thought you have is a projection within your awareness. You contain the universe because your true self—the aware entity—is part of the infinite source.

This idea isn't limited to philosophy. In physics, **holographic principles** suggest that the entire universe can be encoded within any part of it. In other words, each fragment contains the whole, much like a hologram.

The Infinite Potential Within You

Infinity isn't just about the vastness of the cosmos; it's also about your inner potential. Every possibility, every version of you, already exists in the infinite field of consciousness.

The only limits you experience are the ones you impose on yourself. When you recognise your infinite nature, you begin to understand that you are capable of far more than you've been led to believe.

Exercise: Visualising Your Infinite Self

- Find a quiet space and close your eyes.
- Imagine yourself as a vast, expansive field of light, stretching infinitely in all directions.
- Feel the connection between your individual self and the greater universe.

Practising this regularly can help you tap into your boundless potential.

Infinity and Time

Infinity doesn't just apply to space—it also applies to time. We tend to think of time as a linear sequence, but in the grand scheme of things, past, present, and future all exist simultaneously.

Consider a book or a film. While you experience the story in a linear fashion, the entire narrative already exists. The same is true for your life. Every possibility, every version of your journey, is already written in the infinite field of consciousness. You are simply moving through it, one moment at a time.

Living with an Infinite Mindset

So, how do you live in alignment with the infinite nature of reality? Here are some guiding principles:

1. **Let Go of Limitation**
   Most of our perceived limitations are self-imposed. By recognising your infinite nature, you can break free from the constraints of fear, doubt, and scarcity.

2. **Embrace Possibility**
   With infinity as your playground, anything is possible. Allow yourself to dream big, knowing that every possibility exists and is within your reach.
3. **Stay Present**
   While infinity encompasses all of time and space, your point of power is always in the present moment. Embrace the now as the gateway to infinite potential.

Infinity in Science and Philosophy

Throughout history, both scientists and philosophers have grappled with the concept of infinity. In mathematics, infinity represents something larger than any number, a concept essential to understanding calculus and geometry. In physics, the idea of infinite universes or dimensions challenges our perception of reality, suggesting that what we experience is only a fraction of what exists.

Philosophers like Baruch Spinoza and Alan Watts have described infinity as the essence of life itself—a boundless, eternal force from which all things emerge and return. Recognising this unbroken connection to infinity invites us to view life not as a series of finite moments but as part of an endless, evolving continuum.

Living Without Limits

Imagine living in a world where limits don't exist. What would you create? Who would you become?

This thought experiment isn't as far-fetched as it seems. Infinity reminds us that the boundaries we perceive—

whether in time, space, or personal potential—are largely constructs of the human mind. By shifting your perspective and embracing the infinite nature of existence, you open the door to possibilities you once thought impossible.

Write down one area of your life where you feel limited. Then ask yourself: What would this look like if no limitations existed? This simple exercise can help uncover hidden opportunities and inspire bold action.

Conclusion: Embracing the Infinite

Infinity is both humbling and empowering. It reminds us of our smallness in the grand scheme of the cosmos while simultaneously affirming our connection to something vast and boundless.

Takeaways from Chapter 11:

Existence is infinite, with no beginning or end. By recognising infinity, you expand your understanding of your limitless potential. Your life is part of an eternal, interconnected whole.

In the next chapter, we'll explore the concept of time—an illusion that helps us navigate the infinite but often traps us in unnecessary limitations.

Chapter 12: Time—The Great Illusion

Time is one of the most fundamental aspects of our experience, yet it's also one of the most misunderstood. We structure our lives around it, measure it, and even fear it. But what if everything you thought you knew about time was an illusion?

In this chapter, we'll explore the nature of time and reveal how it's more flexible—and illusory—than it seems.

The Two Faces of Time

There are two ways we experience time:

1. **Clock Time**
   This is the time we're all familiar with—the hours, minutes, and seconds ticking away on a clock. It's a human invention, designed to divide the eternal now into measurable chunks. Clock time is useful for organising our lives but doesn't reflect the true nature of reality.
2. **Psychological Time**
   This is how we *feel* time. It stretches when we're bored and flies when we're having fun. Unlike clock time, psychological time is fluid, subjective, and deeply tied to our perception.

Mind-Bending Facts About Time and Perception

Here are some astounding truths that challenge our understanding of time:

- **The Sun Is Always 8 Minutes in the Past**
  When you look at the sun, you're not seeing it as it is now but as it was 8 minutes ago. That's how

long it takes for light to travel from the sun to Earth.

- **Some Stars You Can See No Longer Exist** The light from some stars in the night sky has taken millions of years to reach us. In reality, those stars may have already exploded in a supernova or faded away. You're seeing a snapshot of the distant past. This is due to the time it takes the photons to reach your eyes.

These facts reveal that what we perceive as "reality" is often an image of the past. Even the world around you is a delayed projection, filtered through your senses and brain.

Time as a Human Constraint

Think of time as a tool we've created to navigate life. Like the pages of a book, time allows us to experience events in a linear sequence, making sense of the story. But the entire book—the past, present, and future—already exists.

Similarly, a film reel contains the entire movie at once, but we experience it frame by frame. This limitation isn't due to the nature of reality; it's a constraint of our human perception.

Everything Happens at Once

In the broader, cosmic sense, time doesn't flow the way we perceive it. Quantum physics suggests that all moments—past, present, and future—exist simultaneously in the eternal now.

Consider a profound idea: the future isn't something that "happens" to you; it's something you're constantly creating and stepping into. Every decision and intention you set influences which version of the future you'll experience.

The Illusion of Time—Crafting Your Story in the Eternal Now

Time feels linear, moving steadily from past to present to future. Yet, modern science and ancient wisdom suggest that time is a construct of our perception. In reality, everything happens all at once in the eternal now. But how can this be reconciled with our experience of newness, growth, and decay?

Entropy and the Arrow of Time

One way we perceive time's passage is through **entropy**, the principle that in a closed system, disorder tends to increase. Imagine a pristine sandcastle on the beach. Over time, wind and waves erode it until it becomes a shapeless pile of sand. This increasing disorder, or entropy, creates the sense of an irreversible journey from order to chaos.

Entropy gives time its "arrow," the directional flow from low entropy (order, such as a newborn baby) to high entropy (disorder, like an elderly person or a decayed building). Even in a universe where everything fundamentally exists at once, entropy provides the structure for experiencing change and transformation.

The Eternal Film Reel

Think of reality as a film reel. Every scene of the movie—beginning, middle, and end—already exists. From the projector's perspective, it's all present simultaneously. But when you watch the movie, you experience it frame by frame, creating a sense of time and progression.

Here's where it gets fascinating: although the film is already complete, the experience of the story is shaped by your focus and engagement. Similarly, while all possibilities exist in the field of consciousness, your choices determine which frames you focus on and bring to life.

Are We Living a Predetermined Life?

A natural question arises: If everything happens at once, is the future already written? Are we merely passengers in a predetermined cosmic script?

The answer is both comforting and empowering: no. While all potential outcomes exist simultaneously, you are the director of your personal story. Your thoughts, intentions, and actions determine how the script unfolds.

Imagine standing at a crossroads with infinite paths stretching out before you. Each path represents a different version of your life, and all paths exist simultaneously. Your choices, however, decide which path you walk and what experiences you bring into your conscious reality.

Free Will in an Infinite Universe

Far from being powerless, you possess the ultimate creative freedom. In every moment, you choose which version of reality to manifest. This is why intention and focus are so powerful—they act as the compass that guides your journey through the infinite possibilities of existence.

Practical Insight:
You might have a dream of becoming an artist, a scientist, or a world traveller. All these versions of you already exist in the infinite field. By focusing your thoughts and actions on one of these realities, you bring it to life.

Entropy as the Canvas for Growth

While entropy creates the appearance of decay and ageing, it also provides a fertile ground for growth and evolution. Without the arrow of time, experiences would lack meaning and progression. The beauty of life lies in its transitions—from youth to maturity, from chaos to clarity, from fear to love.

Each change, marked by entropy, allows you to appreciate the richness of existence. The sandcastle may crumble, but its eventual return to the sand reminds us of the cyclical nature of life and the infinite opportunities for creation.

The Dance Between Fate and Free Will

Think of life as a dance between fate (the existence of infinite possibilities) and free will (your ability to choose). The dance floor is always there, filled with every potential step you could take. But the choreography? That's entirely up to you.

This dynamic interplay ensures that while the universe holds infinite outcomes, your unique journey remains a creative process. The story is yours to tell, and the ending is yours to shape.

Directing Your Timeless Movie

Time, as we perceive it, is a tool—a narrative device that allows us to experience the unfolding of life. Entropy provides the structure for this unfolding, marking the transitions and changes that make life meaningful.

But never forget: you are both the protagonist and the director. While the entire reel of your life may already exist, how you experience it is entirely up to you. Your consciousness holds the pen, ready to craft each chapter as it unfolds in the eternal now. The magic lies in how consciousness allows you to experience these scenes one frame at a time, creating a beautiful, unfolding narrative. It's a cosmic illusion—a dance within eternity that lets you savour the journey, step by step, while remaining forever anchored in the infinite present.

Einstein's Relativity: Time Is Not Absolute

Albert Einstein's theory of relativity changed our understanding of time forever. It revealed that time is not a fixed, universal constant. Instead, it's relative and can be stretched or compressed depending on factors like speed and gravity.

For instance, astronauts on the International Space Station age slightly more slowly than people on Earth due to the effects of time dilation. This shows that time is flexible and not the rigid framework we often assume.

Living Beyond the Illusion

So, how can you use this knowledge to transform your life? By recognising that the only real moment is *now*. The past is a memory, the future is a projection, and your point of power lies in the present.

Exercise: Grounding in the Now

- Close your eyes and take a deep breath.
- Bring your attention to the sensations in your body, the sounds around you, and the rhythm of your breath.
- Remind yourself that this moment is all there ever truly is.

Practising presence helps you break free from the anxiety of the future and the regrets of the past, aligning you with the eternal now where your true power resides.

Embrace the Timeless Reality

Time may be an illusion, but it's a useful one—helping us navigate the human experience while reminding us of the deeper, timeless truth. By embracing the present moment and recognising the fluid nature of time, you can live more fully, creatively, and freely.

Takeaways from Chapter 12:

Time is a human construct for navigating the eternal now. Focus on the present moment, where all creation and transformation occur. Linear time is a limitation of perception, not of reality.

In the next chapter, we'll explore vibration—the frequency at which reality resonates—and how aligning with higher frequencies can transform your life.

Chapter 13: Vibration—The Frequency of Reality

The Science of Vibration

Everything in the universe is energy, vibrating at its unique frequency. What appears to be solid is, in fact, a dance of particles in constant motion. This principle applies to the world around you, and even within you—your thoughts, emotions, and physical body.

But how does this vibration affect your life? To understand, we turn to the groundbreaking experiments of Dr. Masaru Emoto.

Dr. Masaru Emoto's Water Experiments

In the late 1990s, Dr. Emoto conducted experiments demonstrating the impact of thoughts, words, and emotions on water. He exposed water samples to various stimuli: positive words like *love* and *gratitude*, and negative ones like *hate* or *fear*.

After freezing the water and examining the crystals under a microscope, the results were astonishing:

- Water exposed to positive words formed beautifully intricate and symmetrical crystals.
- Water exposed to negative words produced chaotic, distorted, and fragmented shapes.

What This Means for You

Given that the human body is about 60% water, your thoughts and emotions profoundly influence your physical and emotional well-being. Every thought you hold sends ripples through your internal energy, shaping the reality you experience.

Your Vibration Shapes Your Reality

You've heard the saying, *Like attracts like.* This principle, rooted in the law of vibration, explains why your internal state—your thoughts and emotions—plays a crucial role in shaping your external reality.

When you vibrate at higher frequencies, resonating with emotions like love, joy, and gratitude, you naturally attract experiences that match those states. Conversely, lower frequencies like fear, anger, or resentment draw more negativity into your life.

The Healing Power of Sound

Sound and vibration have been used for healing for centuries, from ancient chanting practices to modern sound baths.

Healing Frequencies You Can Explore:

- **528 Hz**: Known as the "Love Frequency," this tone is associated with DNA repair, promoting physical and emotional healing.
- **432 Hz**: Revered for its harmony with the natural vibration of the universe, it's said to promote peace and balance.

Many people report a sense of calm and alignment after listening to music or tones tuned to these frequencies. Try incorporating sound therapy into your routine to boost your vibrational health. Sound is a force that resonates through every part of our being, shaping our emotions, health, and overall well-being. The vibrations of sound interact with us on a deep level, creating harmony within and helping to restore balance to both mind and body.

Whether through music, chanting, or intentional sound therapy, these vibrations can have transformative effects, promoting healing, clarity, and even abundance. Sound isn't just a backdrop to life—it's a dynamic energy that connects us to our inner selves and the world around us. By tapping into its power, we can cultivate greater well-being, emotional balance, and alignment with the life we wish to create.

Aligning your vibration with specific frequencies, such as the "Love Frequency" of 528 Hz mentioned earlier, is a practice that blends sound, intention, and awareness. This frequency is often associated with healing, harmony, and emotional balance. One of the simplest ways to connect with it is by listening to music or tones tuned to 528 Hz, easily found on the internet or through apps specialising in sound therapy. You might also explore binaural beats, which use slightly different frequencies in each ear to create a perceived synchronisation in the brain, encouraging relaxation and focus.

For a more tactile approach, tuning forks calibrated to specific frequencies can help you feel the vibrations directly in your body. Combining these tools with deep breathing or mindfulness amplifies their effects, allowing you to feel more centred and aligned. Whether you hum or chant along with the tones, spend time in nature while listening, or simply focus on gratitude as the sounds play, these practices invite a deeper connection to your body and the world around you. By experimenting with what resonates, you'll discover that these frequencies not only uplift your mood but also harmonise your energy, opening new pathways for balance and growth.

Anecdote:

My sister, Sarah, is a testament to the incredible potential of sound as a healing tool. After overcoming major life-threatening health challenges, she discovered the power of sound vibration in her own recovery journey. She has since developed unique sound healing retreats designed to help others experience the profound benefits of this practice. If you're interested in learning more, I encourage you to explore her work at www.lifesong.co.uk.

Thoughts: The Architects of Your Reality

Your thoughts are vibrational signals that constantly shape your life. Repeated thoughts form beliefs, which in turn become your reality. Take a moment to consider: What thoughts are you broadcasting to the universe? Are they aligned with your highest goals and aspirations?

Practical Tip: Whenever you catch yourself in a negative thought spiral, pause and replace those thoughts with positive affirmations. This small shift can have a profound impact on your vibrational state and, ultimately, your reality.

Living in Tune with the Universe

When you align your vibration with your desires, you're essentially tuning into the "station" of the life you want to live. The universe responds to this alignment, delivering experiences and opportunities that resonate with your frequency. It's a process that requires mindfulness and intention, but the rewards are transformative.

Conclusion: The Universe Is a Symphony

The universe operates like an orchestra, with every particle, emotion, and intention contributing to a grand symphony. By tuning your frequency to align with love, abundance, and joy, you play your part beautifully, creating harmony in your life and the world around you.

Takeaways from Chapter 13:

Everything vibrates at specific frequencies, shaping the quality of life experiences. Aligning with higher frequencies attracts positivity, health, and abundance Your thoughts and emotions directly influence your vibrational state.

In the next chapter, we'll explore the cosmic origins of your physical self, diving into the awe-inspiring truth that you are quite literally made of stardust.

Chapter 14: Stardust and Borrowed Atoms

Take a moment to look at your hands. Every atom in your body, from the calcium in your bones to the iron in your blood, was forged in the heart of an ancient star. You are, quite literally, made of stardust.

This isn't just poetic—it's scientific fact. But it's also profoundly spiritual, connecting you to the cosmos in a way that transcends time and space. Let's explore the cosmic dance of atoms and what it means for your life.

The Stardust Connection

Around 13.8 billion years ago, the universe was born in a massive explosion of energy and matter—the Big Bang. Over time, this matter coalesced into stars, which lived, burned, and eventually died in spectacular explosions known as supernovas.

These supernovas scattered their enriched guts—elements like carbon, oxygen, and iron—into the universe. These elements formed new stars, planets, and eventually... *you.*

Mind-Blowing Fact: Every atom in your body has existed for billions of years and has been part of countless other forms before you. You are the cosmos experiencing itself as a human, if only for a short while.

Your Body Is a "New" You Every Seven Years

Throughout your life, your body undergoes a constant process of transformation. You may look in the mirror and notice the changes—your hair turning grey, your skin wrinkling, your muscles weakening. But while your physical form changes with time, something deeper remains unchanged: your sense of "being" or awareness. This core essence of who you are—the observer of your thoughts and experiences—doesn't age, tire, or get scratched by time.

From childhood through old age, your body is in a constant state of flux. Cells die and are replaced, bones regenerate, and even the water in your body is replaced regularly. In fact, the cells of your body renew themselves on a regular cycle, and most of your body is completely renewed every seven years. This means that you are literally a "new" you, cell by cell, roughly once a decade.

Yet, despite this constant regeneration, the core of who you are—your consciousness, your sense of self—remains the same. Whether you're a child, a young adult, or an elderly person, the awareness that you have of your existence is always present, never tired, never worn out, and never "scratched" by the passage of time.

Even though your body changes continuously, you experience a sense of continuity in your awareness. You were once a baby, and now you are an adult, but the essence of your conscious experience—the "you" that perceives life—remains the same. This suggests that consciousness, the very thing that experiences the world, is not bound by the physical state of your body. Your sense of being is a timeless, unchanging thread that weaves through every stage of your physical existence.

Now, let's dive deeper into the atoms that make up your body. The atoms in your body are not as "yours" as you might think. In fact, the atoms that make up your body have been around for billions of years. They have been part of other forms of life, and they have travelled through the universe long before you were born.

Atoms are constantly recycled through the processes of life, death, and decay, meaning that the particles that form your body have passed through countless other beings and environments. Your body is a temporary gathering of atoms—borrowed from the earth, the sky, the oceans, and from beings who lived and died long before you. Despite the fact that your body is constantly in flux, the timeless essence of "you"—your awareness—remains constant, transcending the constant cycle of atom recycling.

This brings us to an important question: if our physical bodies are constantly changing and our atoms have been recycled over aeons, what is it that remains the same? What is it that connects all of our experiences, from childhood to old age, if not consciousness itself?

The answer may be that consciousness, much like the atoms it interacts with, is eternal and ever-present. It doesn't age, tire, or get replaced—it is the constant in a universe of change. And just as your body is a temporary collection of atoms borrowed from the world around you, your consciousness might be a fundamental, timeless force that transcends physical life and connects you to the greater fabric of existence.

Borrowed Atoms: A Cosmic Recycling Programme

The atoms in your body aren’t static. They’re constantly being exchanged with the environment. Every breath you take, every meal you eat, and every drop of water you drink integrates new atoms into your system while old ones are released.

In a very real sense, your body is a temporary collection of borrowed atoms, all of which have passed through countless other forms—perhaps a dinosaur, a flower, or even another person.

The Infinite Rebirth of Atoms

The continuous recycling of atoms connects you to the entire web of life. It's a reminder of the impermanence of your physical form and the eternity of the energy that composes you.

Even when your current body returns to the earth, its atoms will continue to dance through the cosmos, forming new stars, planets, and perhaps even new life.

Discovering the Real You: A Journey of Elimination

The essence of who you are cannot be defined by the fleeting or the physical. In Indian mysticism, an ancient practice involves discovering what you are by first eliminating what you are not. This process helps reveal the pure, unchanging essence—the real you.

The Illusion of Identity

From birth, we construct an identity based on our body, thoughts, emotions, and experiences. But are these truly "you"? Let's explore:

- **You Are Not Your Body**:
  The body is ever-changing, from childhood to old age. Even if you lose limbs, the you that is aware remains whole and intact.
- **You Are Not Your Thoughts**:
  Thoughts come and go like clouds in the sky.

They arise, linger, and dissolve, yet your awareness remains constant.

- **You Are Not Your Emotions**:
  Emotions are transient, shifting throughout the day. They are experiences, not the experiencer.

Exercise: The Elimination Meditation

Purpose: To strip away layers of false identity and connect with the essence of your being.

Steps:

1. **Find a Quiet Space**: Sit comfortably and close your eyes.
2. **Body Awareness**: Focus on your body. Acknowledge its presence, but remind yourself: I am not this body.
3. **Thought Observation**: Notice your thoughts. Observe them without attachment, repeating: I am not these thoughts.
4. **Emotional Awareness**: Tune into your current emotions. Recognise them as fleeting, and affirm: I am not these emotions.
5. **Sink Into Pure Awareness**: As you let go of these layers, notice what remains—the still, silent awareness that observes it all. This is the real you.

The Realisation of Being

When you eliminate all that you are not, what remains is a sense of pure existence—an unchanging, timeless awareness. This essence is not confined by your physical form or mental states. It is the core of your being, connected to the infinite consciousness that underpins all reality.

Reflection:
Spend a few minutes daily reflecting on this practice. Over time, it can help you disidentify from the transient aspects of life, fostering a deeper sense of peace and connection to your true self.

The Spiritual Significance of Stardust

This cosmic perspective isn't just fascinating—it's deeply empowering. It reminds us that we are not separate from the universe but an intrinsic part of it.

Ancient spiritual traditions have long echoed this truth. In Hindu philosophy, the phrase *Tat Tvam Asi* translates to "Thou art that," meaning you are not separate from the divine; you are the divine.

Modern science, with its revelations about stardust and cosmic interconnectedness, offers a new lens to understand this ancient wisdom.

The Sun and Your Heart: A Cosmic Dialogue

The connection between you and the cosmos goes beyond shared atoms—it extends to the very rhythms of life. The sun, our life-giving star, sends out an electromagnetic pulse every moment of every day. This pulse, travelling at the speed of light, reaches Earth, touching every living being.

Remarkably, your heart responds to this pulse. Like a cosmic call-and-response, the sun's electromagnetic rhythm syncs with your heartbeat, creating a subtle but profound connection.

It's as if the sun is asking, *"Are you out there, my child?"* and your heart replies, *"Yes Mother, alive and well."* This isn't just poetic—it's measurable.

Studies in heliobiology have shown that solar activity influences the human cardiovascular system, affecting everything from heart rate to overall well-being.

The Heart's Electromagnetic Field

Your heart isn't just a pump—it's also a powerful electromagnetic organ, generating a magnetic field that extends several feet beyond your body. This field interacts with the Earth's magnetic field and, in turn, with the magnetic pulses of the sun.

When your heart is in a state of coherence—aligned with positive emotions like love and gratitude—its magnetic field becomes more harmonious, enhancing your connection to the cosmic rhythms.

Living in Harmony with the Cosmos

Understanding this connection invites you to live in greater alignment with the universe's natural rhythms. By cultivating heart coherence through practices like meditation, deep breathing, and gratitude, you not only improve your well-being but also strengthen your bond with the cosmos.

Awe as a Gateway to Higher Vibration

Understanding your stardust origins can evoke a profound sense of awe. This emotion, often triggered by the vastness of the universe or the beauty of nature, has been shown to raise your vibrational state.

Practical Exercise: Stardust Meditation

1. Find a quiet space and close your eyes.
2. Visualise the stars, galaxies, and cosmic explosions that created the elements in your body.
3. Feel the connection between your physical self and the universe.
4. Affirm: *I am a unique expression of the cosmos, eternally connected to all that is.*

Living with a Cosmic Perspective

When you see yourself as a part of the universe's infinite cycle, life's challenges and uncertainties take on a new context. You are here for a fleeting moment in cosmic time, but your essence—your energy—will continue to exist, flowing through the fabric of reality.

This understanding invites you to live more fully, appreciate the present moment, and embrace your role as a co-creator in the grand cosmic story.

Conclusion: You Are the Universe

You are more than flesh and bone. You are stardust, temporarily formed into a human being, connected to the infinite dance of the cosmos. By recognising this truth, you can step into your power, knowing that you are as vast, ancient, and limitless as the universe itself.

Takeaways from Chapter 14:

You are made of the same elements as stars, connecting you to the cosmos. Atoms in your body are borrowed from the universe and have a cosmic history. Recognise the miracle of being both a finite body and an infinite consciousness.

Chapter 15: Nature's Pharmacy—Nourishing Body and the Planet

In our journey toward conscious living, the choices we make about what we eat play a pivotal role. Our dietary habits not only influence our personal health but also impact the well-being of our planet. By making mindful food choices, we can elevate our vibrational energy and contribute to a more harmonious world.

The Vibrational Energy of Food

Every food carries a unique vibrational frequency, which can affect our body's energy levels. High-vibration foods, typically fresh, organic and unprocessed, are believed to enhance our vitality and well-being. Conversely, low-vibration foods, often heavily processed or derived from sources involving animal suffering, may diminish our energy.

"You Are What You Eat": The Science Behind the Saying

The adage "you are what you eat" holds substantial truth. Our bodies are constructed from the nutrients we consume, and our diet directly influences our physical and mental health. For instance, diets rich in processed foods and high in refined sugars have been linked to increased risks of obesity, diabetes, and mood disorders.

On the other hand, consuming a diet abundant in whole, plant-based foods provides essential vitamins, minerals, and antioxidants that support optimal bodily functions and mental clarity. Research indicates that individuals who consume more fruits and vegetables experience higher levels of well-being and lower rates of depression.

Nourish and Flourish: Tuning into High-Vibration Foods

Imagine your diet as a music chart, where each food item hits a different note on the vibrational scale. At the top, we have the chart-toppers—the "greatest hits" that energise and uplift. As we move down, the tunes become more eclectic, catering to varied tastes. And at the bottom, we encounter the heavy, intense beats that might leave you feeling drained. Let's explore this symphony of sustenance:

Top-Tier Vibrational Foods: The Greatest Hits

- **Leafy Greens and Vegetables: The Soulful Ballads of Nutrition**: Imagine leafy greens and vibrant vegetables as the soulful ballads in your dietary playlist, each note resonating with life-enhancing energy. These foods are rich in chlorophyll, essential vitamins, and minerals that harmonise with your body's natural rhythms, supporting cellular health and elevating your vibrational frequency. The deep hues of purple vegetables for instance, are due to anthocyanins—powerful antioxidants that combat oxidative stress and inflammation, promoting heart and brain health. By incorporating these high-vibration foods into your meals, you not only nourish your body but also align with a conscious lifestyle that raises your overall energy and well-being hitting all the right notes.

- **Fresh Fruits**: Think of berries, apples, and citrus as the pop anthems of nutrition—bursting with life force, packed with vitamins, antioxidants, and natural sugars. Their high water content hydrates and detoxifies, keeping you dancing through the day.
- **Nuts and Seeds**: Almonds, walnuts, chia, and flaxseeds are the classic rock tracks—concentrated sources of healthy fats, proteins, and energy. These nutrient-dense powerhouses fuel both body and mind, keeping your rhythm steady.
- **Herbs and Spices: The Upbeat Rhythms of Your Culinary Playlist**: Think of herbs and spices like turmeric, ginger, and basil as the lively beats of your dietary soundtrack. They don't just add flavor; they infuse your meals with vibrant energy and healing properties, boosting your immune system and enhancing overall well-being. Incorporating these zestful elements into your dishes can transform your culinary experience into a harmonious symphony of taste and health.

Middle of the Chart: An Eclectic Mix

- **Whole Grains**: Brown rice, quinoa, and oats are the indie tracks—nutrient-rich with a moderate vibrational beat. They provide sustenance but can be heavier to digest, appealing to those with a taste for the unique.
- **Legumes**: Beans and lentils are the folk tunes of the food world, offering protein and fiber. Their vibrational impact varies with preparation and freshness, making them versatile players in your dietary playlist.
- **Fish & Seafood**: Often considered a nutritious alternative to meat, can be likened to jazz fusion—

a genre celebrated for its complexity and richness. However, just as jazz fusion's intricate compositions may not resonate with everyone, the health benefits of fish and seafood are increasingly overshadowed by environmental concerns. Industrial pollution, agricultural runoff, and microplastics have contaminated many aquatic ecosystems, leading to the accumulation of harmful substances like mercury and polychlorinated biphenyls (PCBs) in fish tissues. This situation introduces dissonant notes into the once harmonious perception of fish as a healthful choice, highlighting the need for careful consideration of seafood sources to ensure both personal health and environmental sustainability.

Low-Vibration Foods: The Heavy Metal

- **Dairy Products**: The melancholic tunes—providing calcium and protein but often challenging to digest. Dairy often comes from animals subjected to intense farming practices, lowering its vibrational energy and leaving you feeling out of tune.
- **Meats (Beef, Pork, Lamb, Chicken)**: These are the heavy metal tracks—intense and energetically dense. While meat can be a source of protein, its vibrational energy is generally lower, especially if the animals were raised in stressful, confined conditions. The stress and fear experienced by the animal can imprint energetically, which some believe is passed on to the consumer.
- **Processed Foods:** Imagine processed foods as the chaotic riffs of a death metal track—intense, jarring, and not for the faint-hearted. Packed with

artificial additives, preservatives, and refined sugars, these culinary rebels lack the harmonious life force that nourishes your body. Consuming them can disrupt your body's natural rhythm, leading to fatigue, imbalance, and, in extreme cases, an early encore performance in the afterlife. So, unless you're aiming for a mosh pit in your metabolism, it might be wise to keep these headbangers off your plate.

By curating your dietary playlist with high-vibration "greatest hits," you can create a harmonious balance that resonates with your body's natural rhythm, leading to a more vibrant and energetic life. Your body is a finely tuned energy system, and the food you consume plays a crucial role in how you feel physically, emotionally, and spiritually.

Gentle Steps Toward Conscious Eating

Transitioning to a more plant-based diet doesn't require an all-or-nothing approach. Small, mindful changes can lead to significant benefits:

- **Incorporate More Plant-Based Meals**: Start by introducing one or two vegetarian meals per week. Explore new recipes and discover plant-based foods you enjoy.
- **Choose Quality Over Quantity**: If you consume meat, opt for sources that prioritise animal welfare and sustainable practices.
- **Practise Mindful Eating**: Pay attention to how different foods make you feel. Notice the energy levels and mood changes associated with your dietary choices.

By making conscious food choices, we not only nourish our bodies but also contribute to the health of our planet. Embracing a diet rich in high-vibration foods can elevate our personal energy and foster a deeper connection with the world around us.

Takeaways from Chapter 15:

The quality of the food you eat impacts your physical health and vibrational energy. Responsible, conscious eating supports both personal well-being and planetary health. Nature provides everything needed for healing and thriving.

In the next chapter, we'll explore how this interconnected reality resembles a grand matrix and how consciousness is the key to navigating and shaping it.

Chapter 16: Welcome to the Matrix—Cracking the Code of Reality

Imagine waking up in a world where everything you see, touch, and experience is part of a grand, interconnected system. In this world, reality isn't as solid as it seems. It's more like a digital simulation—a matrix—crafted by consciousness itself.

But unlike the dystopian world of science fiction, this matrix isn't something to fear. It's a dynamic, living framework where you are the architect, capable of shaping your experience with the power of your awareness.

The Illusion of Solidity

Modern science tells us that matter, which feels so real and solid, is mostly empty space. At the atomic level, particles vibrate within vast gaps, held together by energy fields. This illusion of solidity is a construct of your senses, a carefully crafted perception designed to help you navigate the physical world.

But if reality is not as solid as it seems, what is it? The answer lies in consciousness.

Consciousness as the Core Code

In this matrix, consciousness is the fundamental "operating system" from which everything arises. Think of it as the underlying code running the program of reality.

Just as a computer simulation responds to input, your reality responds to your thoughts, emotions, and intentions. What you focus on and believe becomes the code that shapes your experience.

The Brain as a Virtual Reality Interface

Your brain plays a crucial role in this matrix. Acting as an interface, it filters and processes the vast field of consciousness into the manageable reality you perceive.

Remember the radio analogy from earlier? The brain doesn't generate consciousness; it tunes into specific frequencies, allowing you to experience life in this physical dimension.

Looking for consciousness inside the brain is like searching for the characters inside a video game console. The brain is the hardware, translating the infinite potential of consciousness into the immersive experience we call life.

Breaking Free from the Matrix

The most profound realisation in this journey is understanding that you're not just a player in the matrix—you're a creator. Once you grasp this, you can begin to shape your reality intentionally.

Here's how:

1. **Shift Your Focus**
   The matrix responds to your attention. If you focus on fear and limitations, that's what you'll experience. Shift your focus to abundance, love, and possibilities, and watch your reality transform.

2. **Master Your Inner Dialogue**
   Your thoughts are like the code you input into the system. Be mindful of your inner dialogue, replacing limiting beliefs with empowering ones.
3. **Recognise Signs and Synchronicities**
   The matrix communicates with you through signs, coincidences, and patterns. Pay attention to these moments—they're clues guiding you toward your desired reality.

Practical Exercise: Rewriting Your Matrix

- Take a few moments to reflect on an area of your life where you feel stuck.
- Ask yourself: *What thoughts, beliefs, or emotions am I feeding into this situation?*
- Now, rewrite the script. Visualise a new outcome and affirm it as if it's already real. For example, instead of saying, "I hope to find a better job," affirm, "I am thriving in a fulfilling career."

The Matrix and Spiritual Awakening

Many spiritual traditions describe a similar concept to the matrix: the idea that the world we experience is an illusion, or *maya*. The goal of awakening is to see through this illusion and recognise your true nature as infinite consciousness.

The beauty of this journey is that while the matrix offers structure and challenges, it also provides endless opportunities for growth, creativity, and joy.

Conclusion: Become the Architect

You are not a passive participant in the matrix—you are its architect. By understanding the rules of this grand simulation and aligning your thoughts, emotions, and actions with your highest intentions, you can create a life of purpose, connection, and fulfilment.

Takeaways from Chapter 16:

Think of reality as a "customisable program"—your thoughts and beliefs are the code. Life is not something that happens to you; it's something you shape with your awareness. Just like in a video game, you can choose your path by changing how you perceive and respond to challenges.

In the next chapter, we'll explore how to harness the full power of manifestation, turning your desires into tangible reality.

Chapter 17: Manifest Like a Pro—Consciousness Hacks for Life Mastery

By now, you've learned that consciousness is the foundation of reality, and that you are a co-creator in this vast, interconnected matrix. But how do you take these insights and turn them into tangible results? Welcome to the art and science of manifestation.

Manifestation isn't just about wishing for something and hoping it appears. It's about aligning your thoughts, emotions, and actions with the reality you want to create. It's about consciously hacking the matrix to bring your desires into being.

Manifestation: The Basics

At its core, manifestation is the process of turning an idea or intention into reality. This isn't magic or coincidence; it's a natural outcome of aligning your vibrational frequency with your goals.

The universe is like a giant algorithm, constantly responding to your input. When your thoughts, beliefs, and emotions align with your desires, you create a resonance that attracts those desires into your life.

Step 1: Set a Clear Intention

Clarity is key. The universe can't deliver what you want if your signal is fuzzy. Be specific about your goals and desires. Instead of saying, *I want to be successful*, define what success looks like for you: *I am thriving in my dream job, earning £100,000 a year, and loving every moment of it.*

Pro Tip: Use present-tense affirmations to set your intention. This reinforces the belief that your desired reality is already unfolding.

Step 2: Believe It Before You See It

One of the biggest hurdles in manifestation is doubt. It's easy to think, *I'll believe it when I see it.* But the truth is, you must believe it first to see it.

This requires reprogramming your subconscious mind, which often holds limiting beliefs inherited from society, family, or past experiences.

Affirmations and Visualisation:

- Repeat affirmations daily that align with your desired reality.
- Close your eyes and visualise yourself living that reality. Engage all your senses—see, hear, feel, and even smell the details.

Step 3: Align Your Actions

Manifestation is not about sitting back and waiting for the universe to do all the work. It's a co-creative process. Once you've set your intention and raised your vibration, you need to take inspired action.

Example: If your goal is to start a business, research your market, create a plan, and network with potential partners. The universe loves action—it's a signal that you're serious about your desires.

Step 4: Trust the Process

Patience and trust are vital. The universe operates on its own timeline, often orchestrating events behind the scenes to bring your desires into reality. Sometimes, what feels like a delay is actually perfect timing, aligning circumstances in ways you couldn't predict.

Anecdote:
Remember the story of the British racing green BMW? I didn't receive it the day I set my intention, but the universe didn't forget. Five years later, the exact car appeared at the perfect moment. This taught me to trust the process and stay open to unexpected opportunities.

Overcoming Obstacles

Even with the best intentions, obstacles will arise. These are not signs that your manifestation isn't working but opportunities for growth and alignment.

Reframe Challenges: Instead of seeing setbacks as failures, view them as lessons. Ask yourself, *What can I learn from this? How can I adjust my approach?*

Release Resistance: Sometimes, our own fears and doubts create resistance. Practising mindfulness and self-compassion can help you let go of these blocks.

Exercise: The Daily Manifestation Journal

1. **Morning Intention**: Write down your key intention for the day.
2. **Gratitude Practice**: List three things you're grateful for.

3. **Evening Reflection**: Note any signs, synchronicities, or progress toward your goals.

By maintaining a manifestation journal, you'll stay focused and attuned to the small, often miraculous ways the universe supports your journey.

Manifestation Myths Debunked

1. **Manifestation is Just Positive Thinking**
   Positive thinking is a piece of the puzzle, but manifestation requires alignment in thought, emotion, and action.
2. **You Can Manifest Anything Instantly**
   While rapid manifestations are possible, most require time, patience, and consistent effort.
3. **Manifestation Only Works for Big Goals**
   You can manifest small joys and everyday miracles, from finding a great parking spot to having a meaningful conversation.

Conclusion: Become a Manifestation Master

Manifestation is your superpower. By mastering your thoughts, emotions, and actions, you can create a life that aligns with your deepest desires. The universe is your co-creator, always ready to respond to your intentions.

Takeaways from Chapter 17:

Manifestation is about aligning your thoughts, emotions, and actions. Trust in the process, knowing the universe remembers and delivers in its time. Take inspired action when opportunities arise.

Chapter 18: The Breath of Life—Unlocking Your Vital Energy

Breathing is something we do thousands of times a day, often without giving it a second thought. But the way you breathe has a beneficial impact on your health, energy levels, and mental clarity. Many people unknowingly develop poor breathing habits—short, shallow breaths through the mouth—that leave them feeling tired, anxious, and disconnected.

In this chapter, we'll explore the science and art of breathing, drawing from insights in Stuart Sandeman's brilliant book Breathe In, Breathe Out, to show you how mastering your breath can transform your life.

Why Breathing Matters

Breathing is the most fundamental function of life. It supplies your body with oxygen, the fuel for every cell, and removes carbon dioxide, a waste product. But beyond its physiological role, the breath is a bridge between the body and mind, influencing your physical, emotional, and mental states.

The Problem with Modern Breathing

In today's fast-paced world, many of us develop shallow, quick breathing patterns. This "stress breath" often involves inhaling through the mouth and only filling the upper lungs.

Common Issues with Poor Breathing:

- Increased anxiety and stress
- Reduced oxygen exchange, leading to fatigue
- Imbalanced CO2 levels, affecting focus and sleep quality

Breathing is not just a biological function; it's a gateway to aligning with the universe's natural rhythm. Ancient wisdom and modern science reveal that proper breathing can synchronise us with the Earth's pulse and the cosmic order, enhancing physical and spiritual well-being.

Let's delve deeper into how mastering your breath connects you to the heartbeat of the planet and the infinite energy of the universe.

The Earth's Heartbeat: Schumann Resonance

The Earth emits a natural electromagnetic frequency known as the **Schumann Resonance**, averaging around 7.83 Hz. Often called the Earth's "heartbeat," this frequency has a profound impact on life. Interestingly, it aligns with the **alpha brainwave state** in humans, associated with calmness, creativity, and relaxation.

When we breathe deeply and rhythmically, we synchronise our body's rhythms with this natural frequency, promoting a sense of harmony and balance. This connection to the Earth's pulse reinforces our intrinsic link to the natural world.

Ancient Practices and Universal Rhythm

Breath has been revered as a powerful tool in ancient cultures, often viewed as the bridge between the physical and spiritual realms:

- **Pranayama (Yoga Tradition)**:
  In ancient Indian philosophy, pranayama (breath control) is a means to align individual energy with the cosmic rhythm. Controlled breathing techniques not only calm the mind but also enhance life force (prana), fostering unity with the universe.
- **Qigong (Chinese Tradition)**:
  The ancient Chinese practice of qigong involves coordinated breathing to balance Qi (vital life energy) with the Earth's energy. This practice aims to harmonise the practitioner with the universal flow.

These traditions highlight breathwork as a method of tuning into a higher, universal frequency, fostering both physical health and spiritual growth.

Scientific Insights on Breathing and Rhythm

Modern science supports what ancient traditions have long known. The Schumann Resonance, often referred to as the Earth's natural frequency, is believed to influence human brain activity and circadian rhythms.

Benefits of Aligning with Natural Frequencies:

- Improved sleep quality
- Enhanced focus and mental clarity
- Reduction in stress and anxiety

Breathing Techniques for Synchronisation:
Deep, controlled breathing promotes heart-brain coherence—a state where the heart and brain operate in synchrony, improving emotional resilience and cognitive function.

Breathing as a Key to Health and Harmony

1. **Nasal Breathing**
    - Breathing through the nose filters, warms, and humidifies the air, optimising oxygen absorption.
    - Nasal breathing also produces **nitric oxide**, a molecule that enhances circulation and immune response.
2. **Diaphragmatic Breathing**
    - Engaging the diaphragm during deep breathing increases oxygen intake and promotes relaxation.
    - This method balances CO2 levels, improving the efficiency of oxygen delivery to cells.

Practical Exercises for Universal Alignment

1. **Schumann Synchronisation Breath**:
    - Sit quietly and focus on your breath.
    - Inhale for 4 seconds, hold for 7 seconds, and exhale for 8 seconds.

- Visualise your breath aligning with the Earth's pulse, creating a sense of harmony and connection.

2. **Nature Breathing**:
    - Spend time in natural settings and consciously sync your breath with the sounds of nature—waves, rustling leaves, or birdsong.
    -
3. **Cosmic Breath Meditation**:
    - Close your eyes and imagine yourself breathing in universal energy. With each inhale, draw in vitality and connection; with each exhale, release tension and fear.

The Breath as a Cosmic Connector

Breath is not only vital for life but also a profound connector to the larger rhythms of the universe. By practising conscious breathing, you tap into the flow of the Earth's heartbeat and the infinite energy of the cosmos, unlocking your full potential for health, peace, and spiritual growth.

Takeaways from Chapter 18:

Proper correct breathing nourishes your body, mind, and soul. Conscious breathwork can lower stress, improve health, and elevate your vibration. Effortless breathing connects you to the universal rhythm of life.

Chapter 19: The Gratitude Effect—Unlocking Abundance

Gratitude is often overlooked in its simplicity, but it holds a hidden power. It's more than just saying "thank you" for life's blessings. Gratitude is a state of being, a vibrational frequency that aligns you with the energy of abundance.

When you cultivate gratitude, you're not only acknowledging what you have; you're also opening the door for more. Gratitude shifts your focus from what's missing to what's present, creating a fertile ground for manifesting even greater joy, love, and success.

The Science Behind Gratitude

Gratitude isn't just a feel-good emotion—it has measurable benefits for your mental and physical well-being.

Research in **positive psychology** has shown that gratitude:

- Reduces stress and anxiety
- Enhances sleep quality
- Strengthens the immune system
- Increases overall happiness and life satisfaction

In one study, participants who kept a daily gratitude journal reported higher levels of optimism and fewer physical symptoms of illness compared to those who didn't.

Gratitude as a Vibration Booster

In terms of energy, gratitude is one of the highest vibrational states you can achieve. When you're grateful, your heart's electromagnetic field becomes more coherent, amplifying your connection to the universe's abundance.

This coherence is like tuning into a radio station that plays all your favourite songs. When you vibrate at the frequency of gratitude, you naturally attract experiences that match that energy—more opportunities, more joy, more abundance.

Shifting from Lack to Abundance

Many people focus on what they lack, thinking this will motivate them to achieve more. But this mindset keeps you trapped in a low-vibrational state. Gratitude flips the script.

By focusing on what you *already have*, no matter how small, you signal to the universe that you're open to receiving more. It's as if you're saying, *Thank you, I'm ready for even greater blessings.*

Practical Gratitude Exercises

1. **The Gratitude Journal**

Each morning or evening, write down three things you're grateful for.
Be specific: instead of writing, "I'm grateful for my job," say, "I'm grateful for the supportive colleagues and the creative challenges my job offers."

2. **Gratitude Walk**

Take a walk and consciously observe the world around you.
With each step, mentally note something you're thankful for—the warmth of the sun, the beauty of a tree, the rhythm of your breath.

3. **Gratitude Letters**

Write a letter to someone who has positively impacted your life.
Whether you send it or not, the act of expressing gratitude will elevate your vibration.

The Power of Thanking the Future

Gratitude isn't just for the present—it's a powerful tool for manifesting your future. By expressing gratitude for things that haven't yet materialised, you align yourself with the reality where they already exist.

Affirmation Practice:

- Each day, say or write affirmations like, *I am grateful for the financial abundance flowing into my life,* or, *I am thankful for the loving relationships surrounding me.*

This technique shifts your focus from longing to receiving, reinforcing the belief that your desires are on their way.

Gratitude and the Brain

Gratitude rewires your brain. Studies using fMRI scans show that practising gratitude activates the brain's reward system, releasing dopamine and serotonin—the "feel-good" neurotransmitters.

Over time, this strengthens neural pathways associated with positive thinking, making gratitude a natural, automatic response. The more you practise, the easier it becomes to see the silver lining in any situation.

Overcoming Gratitude Blocks

Sometimes, it's hard to feel grateful—especially during challenging times. But even in difficulty, there's always something to appreciate.

Reframe Challenges:

- Ask yourself: *What can I learn from this? How is this experience helping me grow?*
- Even setbacks often carry hidden blessings, like increased resilience or unexpected opportunities.

Start Small:

- On tough days, focus on simple things: clean water, a warm bed, or the support of a friend.

The Ripple Effect of Gratitude

Gratitude doesn't just transform your life—it ripples out to those around you. When you express appreciation, you elevate the mood and energy of others, creating a cycle of positivity and connection.

Imagine a world where more people lived in gratitude. The collective vibration would rise, leading to greater harmony, compassion, and abundance for all.

Conclusion: Gratitude as a Way of Life

Gratitude is more than a practice; it's a way of being. By embracing it, you unlock the full potential of abundance and joy, transforming not just your life but the world around you.

Takeaways from Chapter 19:

Gratitude shifts your focus from what's missing to what's already good in your life. It's like flipping a mental switch that helps you notice the small joys—whether it's a sunny day, a kind word, or a warm cup of tea—and these moments add up to create a sense of abundance. A grateful mindset attracts more abundance and joy into your life. Practicing gratitude creates a ripple effect of positivity around you.

In the next chapter, we'll explore the art of surrender—how letting go can open doors to possibilities beyond your imagination.

Chapter 20: The Art of Surrender—Flowing with Life's Current

In a world that glorifies control and hustle, surrender can feel counterintuitive. We're taught to chase our goals relentlessly, to hold on tightly to our plans. But what if the key to achieving your dreams and living a fulfilled life isn't about control, but about letting go?

Surrender is not about giving up; it's about trusting the flow of life. It's about releasing the need to micromanage every detail and opening yourself to the infinite possibilities the universe offers.

What Does It Mean to Surrender?

Surrender doesn't mean passivity or resignation. It's an active process of aligning with the natural flow of life. When you surrender, you:

- Release resistance to what is.
- Let go of attachment to specific outcomes.
- Trust that the universe has your back, even when things don't go as planned.

Think of surrender as rowing with the current rather than against it. You're still moving forward, but with ease and grace, rather than struggle.

Why Surrender Is Powerful

When you let go of the need for control, you allow the universe to work its magic. Often, the plans we cling to are limited by our human perspective. Surrender opens the door for outcomes that are greater than anything you could have imagined.

Example: You may be fixated on landing a specific job, believing it's the key to your happiness. But by surrendering, you might find yourself in an entirely different role that aligns more deeply with your purpose.

The Link Between Surrender and Manifestation

Surrender is a crucial component of manifestation. Once you've set your intention and taken inspired action, surrender allows the universe to handle the details. Holding on too tightly to your desired outcome can create resistance, blocking the flow of energy.

Personal Anecdote:
In my own life, some of the best opportunities came when I released my attachment to a specific outcome. By surrendering, I created space for unexpected blessings to flow in, often in ways that were far better than my original plan.

Letting Go of Resistance

Resistance often comes in the form of fear, doubt, or the need to control every aspect of your life. But resistance is like swimming upstream—it drains your energy and keeps you stuck.

Signs of Resistance:

- Feeling anxious or frustrated when things don't go as planned.

- Obsessing over outcomes and trying to force solutions.
- Ignoring signs and opportunities because they don't fit your original plan.

How to Release Resistance:

- Practice mindfulness to stay present and grounded.
- Use affirmations like, *I trust the flow of life* or *I release what no longer serves me.*
- Cultivate self-compassion and remind yourself that it's okay to not have all the answers.

The Role of Faith and Trust

Surrender requires faith—not necessarily in a religious sense, but in the belief that the universe is working in your favour. Trust that every experience, even the challenges, is guiding you toward your highest good.

Practical Exercise: The Let-Go List

- Write down anything you're currently trying to control or force—situations, outcomes, or worries.
- Next to each item, write: *I release this to the universe.*
- Reflect on how it feels to let go and trust.

Surrendering to the Present Moment

One of the most powerful forms of surrender is accepting the present moment exactly as it is. Life unfolds in the now, and resisting the present only creates suffering.

When you embrace the present, you tap into the flow of life, where solutions arise naturally, and peace becomes your default state.

When Surrender Feels Difficult

Letting go can be challenging, especially when you're deeply attached to a specific outcome. Here's how to navigate those moments:

- **Acknowledge Your Feelings**: It's okay to feel disappointed or frustrated. Honour those emotions without judgement.
- **Reframe the Situation**: Ask yourself, *What if this is happening for me, not to me?*
- **Focus on What You Can Control**: While you can't control every outcome, you can control your mindset and actions.

The Balance Between Action and Surrender

Surrender doesn't mean sitting back and doing nothing. It's about taking inspired action and then releasing the need to control the outcome. It's a dance between effort and trust, intention and flow.

Imagine planting a seed. You water it, give it sunlight, and nurture it, but you don't dig it up every day to check if it's growing. You trust the process, knowing that nature will take care of the rest.

Conclusion: The Freedom of Surrender

Surrendering to life's flow doesn't mean you lose control—it means you gain freedom. Freedom from unnecessary stress, from the need to force outcomes, and from the illusion that you have to do it all alone.

By surrendering, you align yourself with the universe's wisdom and grace, allowing life to unfold in its most beautiful and harmonious way.

Takeaways from Chapter 20:

Surrendering is not giving up—it's trusting the flow of life. Letting go of control opens doors to unexpected possibilities. Resistance creates struggle; surrender brings peace and clarity.

In the next chapter, we'll explore how your relationships shape your vibrational reality and how to cultivate connections that elevate and empower you.

Chapter 21: The Vibrational Power of Relationships

The Illusion of Separation

One of the most profound implications of consciousness being fundamental is the realisation that we are all deeply connected. While it feels as though each of us is an independent being—separate and unique—this is merely an illusion created by the mind. In reality, we are all expressions of the same universal consciousness, experiencing life through billions of perspectives, including those of animals and other sentient beings.

The part of you that is aware of being aware is the same in every other conscious being. The "I" that observes your thoughts and experiences is not different from the "I" in others. It's as if consciousness is a vast ocean, and each of us is a wave—distinct for a moment, yet inseparably part of the whole.

Timeless Wisdom from Sages

Throughout history, sages and spiritual leaders have pointed to this truth. Jesus encapsulated it beautifully when he said, Whatsoever you do to the least of my brothers, you do unto me. This wasn't just a moral teaching; it was a direct reference to the shared nature of consciousness. When you harm another, you are, in essence, harming yourself. Conversely, acts of kindness, compassion, and love uplift not just the recipient but the collective whole, including you.

The Buddha similarly taught the interconnectedness of all beings, and many indigenous traditions hold that the Earth and its creatures are not separate from us but part of a sacred, unified web of life.

The Implications for Daily Life

Understanding that we are all the same consciousness reshapes how we view relationships, conflicts, and even our impact on the world.

- **Kindness and Compassion**: When you extend kindness to others, you're nurturing the universal consciousness of which you are a part.
- **Empathy**: Recognising that others' pain and joy are not separate from your own fosters deeper empathy.
- **Responsibility**: Every thought, word, and action contributes to the collective experience. By elevating your vibration, you uplift the whole.

Practical Reflection

In moments of conflict or frustration, pause and remind yourself: the other person is another version of you, experiencing life through a different lens. What would change if you approached each interaction with this awareness?

Affirmation:

I am one with all life. Every act of love and kindness I give, I receive in return.

Relationships are a cornerstone of the human experience. They challenge us, inspire us, and shape our vibrational reality. Whether it's a friendship, romantic partnership, or family bond, every connection carries its own energetic signature.

But not all relationships are created equal. Some elevate your vibration, while others drain your energy. The key to thriving in life is learning to cultivate relationships that uplift and support your journey.

The Energy Exchange in Relationships

Every interaction is an exchange of energy. When you spend time with someone, your vibrational states begin to align. This is why you may feel energised after a conversation with a supportive friend or drained after spending time with someone who constantly complains.

Vibrational Alignment:

- High-vibration relationships amplify feelings of love, joy, and abundance.
- Low-vibration relationships can perpetuate fear, anger, or self-doubt.

By becoming aware of these dynamics, you can consciously choose which relationships to nurture and which to distance yourself from.

Recognising Energy Vampires

"Energy vampires" are individuals who, often unknowingly, drain your energy. They might constantly focus on negativity, demand excessive attention, or create drama. While it's important to have compassion, it's equally vital to protect your own vibrational well-being.

Signs of an Energy Vampire:

- You feel exhausted or anxious after interacting with them.
- They rarely offer support or encouragement.
- Conversations are one-sided, revolving around their problems.

How to Protect Your Energy:

- Set clear boundaries.
- Limit your time and emotional investment in these relationships.
- Practise energetic cleansing techniques, such as visualising a protective light around you.

Elevating Your Inner Circle

Surrounding yourself with high-vibration individuals can significantly enhance your life. These are people who:

- Encourage your growth and celebrate your successes.
- Inspire you with their own positive energy and mindset.
- Offer genuine support and constructive feedback.

Practical Exercise: The Relationship Audit

1. Make a list of the key people in your life.
2. Reflect on how each relationship makes you feel—energised, neutral, or drained.
3. Decide which relationships to nurture, which to reframe, and which to release or limit.

The Power of Love and Forgiveness

Love is the highest vibrational state, and forgiveness is its ultimate expression. Holding onto resentment or anger lowers your vibration and keeps you tied to the past. Forgiveness, on the other hand, frees both you and the other person, allowing you to move forward with a lighter heart.

Steps to Forgive:

- Acknowledge your feelings without judgement.
- Recognise that forgiveness is for your benefit, not necessarily for theirs.
- Visualise releasing the negative energy tied to the person or event.

Romantic Relationships as Mirrors

Romantic relationships often serve as powerful mirrors, reflecting both your strengths and areas for growth. They can challenge you to confront your deepest fears and insecurities while offering opportunities for profound connection and healing.

When approached with awareness, these relationships become a sacred space for mutual growth and evolution.

Key Questions for Reflection:

- What is this relationship teaching me about myself?
- How can I bring more love, patience, and understanding into this connection?

Cultivating Conscious Connections

Conscious relationships are built on mutual respect, trust, and a shared commitment to growth. They're not free from challenges, but they thrive on open communication and a willingness to navigate difficulties together.

Qualities of Conscious Relationships:

- Active listening and empathy.
- Clear, honest communication.
- A balance of giving and receiving.

Relationships and the Collective Vibration

Your relationships don't just impact your personal vibration; they contribute to the collective energy of your community and the world. By fostering high-vibration connections, you play a role in raising the collective frequency, creating a ripple effect of positivity and harmony.

Conclusion: Your Vibrational Tribe

The people you surround yourself with have a direct impact on your journey. By cultivating conscious, high-vibration relationships, you create a supportive environment for growth, joy, and abundance.

Takeaways from Chapter 21:

Relationships mirror your own vibrational state. Surround yourself with positive, supportive people to elevate your energy. Authentic, conscious connections enrich your life and align you with higher vibrations.

In the next chapter, we'll dive into the incredible connection between nature and consciousness, exploring how reconnecting with the natural world can elevate your vibration and restore balance in your life.

Chapter 22: Reconnecting with Nature—Your Portal to Higher Consciousness

In the hustle and bustle of modern life, it's easy to forget the connection we have with the natural world. Yet, nature has always been humanity's greatest teacher, healer, and guide. When you step into a forest, walk by the ocean, or even sit in a quiet garden, you're not just enjoying a moment of peace—you're realigning with the very source of life.

Nature is more than a backdrop to our lives; it's a living, breathing portal to higher consciousness.

The Healing Power of Nature

Science now confirms what ancient cultures have always known: spending time in nature has transformative effects on the mind and body.

Studies Show:

- **Reduced Stress and Anxiety**: Simply being in natural surroundings lowers cortisol levels, the hormone associated with stress.
- **Improved Focus and Creativity**: A walk in the park can sharpen your mind and boost your problem-solving abilities.
- **Enhanced Physical Health**: Regular exposure to nature strengthens the immune system, reduces blood pressure, and improves heart health.

The Japanese practice of *shinrin-yoku*, or "forest bathing," involves immersing oneself in a forest's atmosphere. This simple yet hugely beneficial activity has been shown to promote relaxation, improve mood, and even increase life expectancy.

Nature's Hidden Intelligence

Beyond its beauty and tranquillity, nature is a master of adaptation, resilience, and communication.

Mind-Blowing Examples:

- **Mimicking Plants**: Some plants, like the orchid mantis, mimic the appearance of other species to attract pollinators or evade predators. Without eyes or brains, they somehow "know" what to do to survive.
- **The Mycelium Network**: Beneath every forest lies a vast network of fungal threads known as mycelium. This "underground internet" connects trees, allowing them to share nutrients and even warn each other of threats.

These examples challenge our understanding of intelligence and consciousness. If plants and fungi can demonstrate such remarkable abilities without a central nervous system, what does this say about the nature of awareness?

The Vibrational Harmony of Nature

Everything in nature vibrates at a frequency that promotes balance and well-being. When you spend time in these high-frequency environments, your own vibration begins to sync with them, lifting you out of stress and negativity.

The Heart-Nature Connection:
Studies have shown that the electromagnetic field of the human heart aligns with the Earth's magnetic field when we spend time in nature. This alignment creates a state of coherence, enhancing emotional and physical well-being.

It's as if nature gently whispers, *Remember who you are.*

Nature as a Mirror of Consciousness

Nature operates with effortless intelligence. The tides don't struggle to meet the shore; trees don't force themselves to grow. Everything flows in perfect harmony, guided by an unseen but deeply intuitive force.

This is a mirror of your own consciousness. When you stop resisting life and start flowing with it, you tap into the same effortless power that guides the natural world.

Practical Ways to Reconnect with Nature

1. **Daily Micro-Doses of Nature**
   You don't need a forest retreat to reap the benefits of nature. Spend time in a local park, tend to a garden, or simply open a window and listen to the birds.
2. **Mindful Walks**
   Leave your phone behind and take a walk with full presence. Notice the colours, sounds, and textures around you. Feel the ground beneath your feet and the air on your skin.
3. **Nature Meditation**
   Sit in a natural setting and focus on your breath. As you inhale, imagine drawing in the life force of the earth. As you exhale, release any tension or worry, letting it dissolve into the ground.

4. **Forest Bathing**
   Find a wooded area and spend time simply being. No agenda, no goals—just immerse yourself in the sights, sounds, and smells of the forest.

The Wisdom of Seasons

Nature teaches us the power of cycles. Just as the seasons change, so do the phases of our lives. There's a time for growth and expansion, a time for reflection and rest, and everything in between.

By observing and aligning with these natural rhythms, you can navigate life with greater ease and grace.

Nature's Role in Spiritual Awakening

Many spiritual traditions emphasise the importance of connecting with nature as part of awakening. Whether it's through fasting in the desert, meditating in the mountains, or simply walking by a river, nature strips away the distractions of modern life and brings you back to your essence.

In these moments, the boundaries between you and the world dissolve. You feel not as a separate being but as a part of the greater whole. This is the power of nature: it reminds you of your infinite connection to the universe.

Conclusion: A Return to the Source

Nature is your ally, your teacher, and your guide. By reconnecting with it, you realign with the rhythms of life, raising your vibration and deepening your connection to higher consciousness.

Takeaways from Chapter 22:

Nature grounds and restores balance in your life. Immersion in natural environments raises your vibration and deepens awareness. Nature reminds us of our connection to the infinite.

In the next chapter, we'll delve into the transformative power of psychedelics like 5-MeO-DMT, exploring how these natural substances can dissolve the ego and provide a direct experience of the infinite.

Chapter 23: Dissolving the Ego—The Psychedelic Gateway to Infinity

There are moments in life when the boundaries of the self dissolve, and you catch a glimpse of something far greater—a boundless reality where the ego melts away, and you feel deeply connected to everything. Psychedelics, especially natural substances like **5-MeO-DMT, '5-Methoxy-N,N-Dimethyltryptamine'**, have the power to facilitate these transformative experiences, offering a direct encounter with the infinite nature of existence.

In this chapter, we'll explore the profound effects of these substances, their role in spiritual awakening, and the insights they reveal about the true nature of consciousness.

What Is 5-MeO-DMT?

For centuries, cultures around the world have revered certain plants and substances for their ability to dissolve the ego and provide a mystical bridge to the infinite. Among these substances is 5-MeO-DMT, often called the "God molecule" for the transformative experiences it has been known to induce. Found naturally in various plants and even within the human body, this compound has the power to strip away the layers of the ego, unveiling a reality far beyond the ordinary.

When the ego or 'personality' dissolves, what remains is an unfiltered experience of oneness—a direct encounter with the boundless source of all creation. Those who have undergone such journeys describe a world of fractals and infinite patterns, feelings of unconditional love, and the understanding that they are not separate from the universe but part of its fabric. The experience is often likened to "returning home" or remembering something deeply familiar yet long forgotten.

The Mystery of Plant Medicines

Nature seems to provide these substances not as mere chemicals, but as keys to a door hidden within the human psyche. Indigenous cultures have long used plants like ayahuasca, peyote, and iboga in sacred ceremonies, not for recreation, but for healing, spiritual growth, and communion with the divine. These rituals often include intention setting, music, and guidance from experienced shamans, creating a safe and intentional environment for participants to explore the mysteries of their consciousness.

Modern research is beginning to catch up, with studies revealing how psychedelics impact the brain. Neuroimaging shows that substances like 5-MeO-DMT reduce activity in the default mode network (DMN)—the part of the brain responsible for maintaining the ego and self-referential thinking. When this network quiets, the boundaries between "self" and "other" dissolve, allowing for a profound sense of unity and interconnectedness.

A Gateway to the Infinite

What makes these experiences so life changing is their ability to remind us of something universal: we are not just observers in the universe; we are the universe experiencing itself. This shift in perception can have lasting effects, helping people let go of deep-seated fears, grudges, or limiting beliefs. The feeling of being "part of everything" transcends cultural, religious, and scientific boundaries, pointing to a truth that words can only partially capture.

While the mechanism of action remains a mystery, the insight gained from these journeys aligns with the teachings of many ancient philosophies. From the Hindu concept of Atman (the true self) to the Zen realisation of "no-self," the dissolution of the ego has always been viewed as a gateway to higher understanding.

A Word of Caution and Wonder

It's important to recognise that while these substances offer incredible insights, they are not for everyone. Their effects can be overwhelming, and without the proper context or guidance, they may lead to confusion or distress. Many people find that practices like meditation, breathwork, or mindfulness can provide similar glimpses into the infinite, offering a gentler path to self-discovery.

The fact that these compounds exist in nature raises profound questions about their purpose. Are they evolutionary tools to expand human consciousness? Or are they a reminder from the natural world of our deep interconnectedness with all that exists? Whatever the answer, their presence invites us to explore the mysteries of our existence with curiosity, respect, and humility.

Insights from Psychedelic Journeys

People who have undergone 5-MeO-DMT experiences frequently describe a monumental shift in their understanding of life and existence. Here are some common insights:

1. **The Illusion of Separation**
   The ego creates the illusion that we are separate individuals, isolated from one another and the universe. Under 5-MeO-DMT, this illusion dissolves, revealing an intense sense of unity.
2. **Death as a Transition**
   Many describe the experience as a kind of "mini-death," where the fear of physical death is replaced by an understanding that consciousness is eternal.
3. **Love as the Fundamental Force**
   At the core of the experience, users often encounter a boundless field of love, which they describe as the essence of all existence.

The Therapeutic Potential

Psychedelics like 5-MeO-DMT are now being explored for their therapeutic benefits, particularly in treating conditions such as depression, anxiety, and PTSD. The ego can trap individuals in patterns of fear, regret, and self-judgement. By temporarily dissolving the ego, these substances

Conclusion: A Glimpse of the Infinite

The experience of ego dissolution through psychedelics like 5-MeO-DMT offers a powerful reminder of our true nature: infinite, interconnected, and rooted in love. While these journeys are profound, they are not the only path to awakening. The same truths can be accessed through meditation, mindfulness, and daily acts of presence.

Takeaways from Chapter 23:

Certain natural substances found in plants hold the mysterious ability to dissolve the ego, offering glimpses of a boundless reality. Ego dissolution unveils a profound connection to the infinite source of all creation, where individuality melts into oneness. These extraordinary substances remind us of the deeper layers of existence and the infinite potential within us.

In the next chapter, we'll explore the concept of multiple selves, diving into the extraordinary phenomena of dissociative identity and how it sheds light on the infinite potential of consciousness.

Chapter 24: Infinite Selves—The Mystery of Multiplicity

What if there wasn't just one self within you, but many? This is the extraordinary reality of individuals with **Dissociative Identity Disorder (DID)**, formerly known as multiple personality disorder. Their experiences challenge our conventional understanding of identity and offer complex insights into the infinite potential of consciousness.

By exploring the mysteries of multiplicity, we uncover how consciousness can manifest in ways that defy the limits of our current scientific and philosophical frameworks.

What Is Dissociative Identity Disorder?

DID is a condition where a person's consciousness fragments into distinct identities, each with its own thoughts, memories, behaviours, and even physical characteristics. These identities, or "alters," can take on unique roles and personalities, often unaware of one another.

DID typically develops as a coping mechanism in response to severe trauma, particularly in childhood. It allows the mind to compartmentalise painful experiences, creating distinct selves to handle different aspects of life.

Mind-Bending Facts About DID

The phenomenon of DID offers some of the most compelling evidence of consciousness's extraordinary capabilities. Here are some of the most astonishing aspects:

1. **Physical Changes Between Alters**
   Alters can exhibit different physical characteristics. For example, one alter may have a different dominant hand, eye colour variations, or even allergies that another alter does not.
2. **Language and Skill Sets**
   Some alters speak different languages or possess skills that others do not, demonstrating a level of compartmentalisation that challenges our understanding of memory and learning.
3. **Changes in Brain Activity**
   Neuroimaging studies show distinct patterns of brain activity corresponding to different alters, suggesting that each identity operates with its own neural pathways.

The Fluid Nature of Identity

The experiences of individuals with DID reveal that identity is far more fluid and malleable than we typically believe. If consciousness can create and sustain multiple, distinct selves within a single body, what does that say about the nature of self?

It suggests that who we are—our sense of "I"—is not fixed. Instead, it's a construct that consciousness shapes and reshapes in response to our experiences and environment.

Multiplicity in Everyday Life

While DID is an extreme example, the concept of multiple selves applies to all of us. Think about how you behave in different roles:

- You might be confident and assertive at work, but playful and relaxed with friends.
- You might show patience and understanding as a parent but exhibit a competitive edge during sports.

These shifts in behaviour and identity illustrate the natural multiplicity within us all. Consciousness adapts, taking on different "selves" to navigate the complexities of life.

The Spiritual Implications of Multiplicity

In spiritual traditions, the concept of multiplicity is not new. Many teachings describe the human experience as a dance of various aspects of the self, ultimately aiming to transcend these roles and connect with the higher, unified self.

DID offers a unique lens through which to explore these spiritual truths. It shows that the boundaries of identity are flexible and that consciousness has the capacity to manifest in myriad forms.

Lessons from Multiplicity

1. **Identity Is a Tool, Not a Fixed State**
   Your identity is not who you are; it's a tool your consciousness uses to interact with the world. Understanding this can help you let go of limiting beliefs and embrace your infinite potential.

2. **Healing Through Integration**
   For individuals with DID, healing often involves bringing their various alters together into a cohesive and unified sense of self. Similarly, personal growth requires embracing all aspects of your identity—your strengths, your vulnerabilities, and the parts of yourself that you may avoid or struggle to accept. These less acknowledged parts, sometimes referred to as "shadows," hold valuable lessons and insights that can lead to greater self-awareness and wholeness.
3. **The Infinite Potential of the Mind**
   The extraordinary abilities of individuals with DID highlight the mind's limitless potential. If consciousness can create multiple identities, each with its own distinct characteristics, what else might it be capable of?

Expanding Your Perspective

The mystery of multiplicity invites you to expand your understanding of self and reality. It challenges you to consider the infinite ways consciousness can express itself, not just within individuals but across the entire spectrum of existence.

Conclusion: Embracing the Many Within

By exploring the phenomenon of multiplicity, we gain a deeper appreciation for the complexity and infinite potential of consciousness. Whether through the lens of DID or the everyday roles we play, we see that identity is a fluid, dynamic expression of the infinite self.

Takeaways from Chapter 24:

Dissociative Identity Disorder highlights the mind's extraordinary ability to create multiple "selves." Each "self" within us—our strengths, fears, and vulnerabilities—can be integrated into a harmonious whole. Exploring your inner multiplicity unlocks hidden potential and greater self-awareness.

In the next chapter, we'll dive into the fascinating connection between fractals and the infinite nature of reality, exploring how these patterns reveal the boundless structure of the universe and consciousness itself.

Chapter 25: Fractals—Patterns of the Infinite

Imagine a world where every part contains the whole, and each layer reveals a deeper complexity, yet mirrors the same pattern. This is the world of **fractals**—mathematical structures that embody the infinite.

Fractals aren't just abstract concepts or beautiful visuals; they are the blueprints of nature, the architecture of reality, a symbol of consciousness itself. Let's explore how these patterns unlock the secrets of infinity and your place within it.

What Are Fractals?

A fractal is a complex geometric shape that can be split into parts, each of which is a reduced-scale copy of the whole. This property, known as **self-similarity**, makes fractals unique. No matter how much you zoom in or out, the pattern remains consistent.

Examples in Nature:

- **Fern Leaves**: Each small leaflet resembles the entire fern.
- **Snowflakes**: Complex patterns repeat on every scale.
- **Rivers and Streams**: Tributaries form smaller versions of the larger river system.

Fractals are nature's way of expressing infinity in the finite world.

The Infinite Nature of Reality

Fractals provide a tangible way to grasp the infinite. While your everyday experiences might suggest that reality is finite, fractals remind us that infinity is all around us. From the vastness of galaxies to the intricacies of DNA, fractal patterns permeate existence.

When people experience states of expanded consciousness, whether through meditation, near-death experiences, or psychedelics like **5-MeO-DMT**, they often report visions of fractals. These patterns seem to represent the infinite, interconnected web of life, offering a glimpse into the deeper structure of reality.

Fractals and the Human Body

The human body itself is a fractal masterpiece. Consider the branching of blood vessels, the structure of lungs, or even the folds of your brain—each mirrors fractal geometry.

This self-similarity ensures efficiency and harmony, allowing life to flourish. It's a reminder that your physical form is not separate from nature but a continuation of its infinite design.

Fractals as a Metaphor for Consciousness

Consciousness operates much like a fractal. Each individual is a unique expression of the universal consciousness, yet we all contain the essence of the whole.

You Are the Universe in Miniature:

- Just as a fractal repeats its pattern at every scale, your consciousness reflects the infinite nature of the source.
- The insights, creativity, and wisdom you access are not confined to your individual mind; they are expressions of the universal consciousness flowing through you.

Fractals and Spiritual Philosophy

Ancient philosophies often hinted at fractal-like principles. The Hermetic axiom, *As above, so below; as within, so without,* aligns perfectly with the concept of self-similarity.

This idea suggests that the microcosm (your inner world) mirrors the macrocosm (the universe). By understanding yourself, you gain insights into the nature of reality itself.

Practical Exercise: Seeing the Infinite in the Everyday

1. **Nature Walk**:
   Take a walk and observe fractal patterns in your surroundings—trees, leaves, clouds. Notice how the same patterns repeat at different scales.
2. **Fractal Meditation**:
   Visualise a fractal pattern, such as the Mandelbrot set. As you focus on its infinite layers, reflect on the boundless nature of your own consciousness.

The Mathematical Beauty of Fractals

Fractals aren't just visual; they're deeply mathematical. One of the most famous fractals, the **Mandelbrot Set**, reveals infinite complexity within a simple formula: **zn+1 =zn2+c**

This formula generates an endless pattern of intricate shapes, highlighting how simple rules can produce infinite complexity—a concept mirrored in the laws of the universe.

The Universe as a Fractal Hologram

Some scientists and philosophers propose that the universe itself may operate as a fractal hologram. In this model, every part of the universe contains the information of the whole, much like a holographic image.

This theory aligns with the idea that your consciousness is not a small, isolated phenomenon but a direct expression of the infinite field of reality.

Conclusion: Embracing the Infinite Within

Fractals offer a profound reminder that infinity is not an abstract concept but an intrinsic part of existence. By recognising the fractal patterns in nature, your body, and your consciousness, you deepen your connection to the infinite source.

Takeaways from Chapter 25:

Fractals are self-repeating patterns found in nature, from the branching of trees and blood vessels to the structure of galaxies, showing how the same principles apply at every scale of the universe. Studies in fractal geometry reveal that these patterns not only make up the physical world but also influence human perception, with fractal visuals having calming effects on the mind. Fractals remind us that life's complexity is not random but follows a deeper, infinite order—one that connects the smallest particles to the vast cosmos.

Chapter 26: The Illusion of Movement—Are We Nearly There Yet?

In our daily lives, movement feels undeniable. We walk, run, fly across continents, and sail across oceans. Yet, if consciousness is truly infinite and fundamental, does it ever actually move? Or is the experience of movement just a grand illusion—a clever trick of perception?

Let's dive into this mind-bending thought experiment and explore how everything, from the distant stars to the cities we travel to, might be appearing within the infinite field of consciousness.

The Omnipresence of Consciousness

Consciousness is often described as omnipresent—meaning it exists everywhere, at all times. If that's true, then it cannot move into a space it doesn't already occupy. Unlike our physical bodies, which seem to traverse distances, consciousness is ever-present, observing all things from a constant state of here and now.

Light and Sound: Reality Comes to You

Consider how we experience the world:

- **Light** travels as photons, entering our eyes, allowing us to perceive objects.
- **Sound** arrives as vibrating waves, stimulating our eardrums.

In both cases, information comes to us, and the brain interprets these signals, creating a cohesive picture of the external world. This means that, even as we perceive objects as "out there," the experience of them is happening within us, in our consciousness.

The Plane Example: Who's Really Moving?

When you board a plane and travel to another country, your senses tell you that you're moving across vast distances. You feel the hum of the engines, see the changing landscapes, and hear the announcements. But what if, instead of you moving, the plane, the destination, and the journey are unfolding within your consciousness?

From this perspective, it's not the body or the plane that moves—it's your perception that shifts, creating the illusion of travel. Consciousness remains static, observing the dynamic play of changing experiences.

Physics Meets Philosophy

1. **Quantum Mechanics**:
   In quantum theory, particles don't exist in a specific location until observed. This principle suggests that physical reality may not be "fixed" but instead arises from observation. If the universe behaves this way on a quantum level, could it also apply to our macro experiences of movement?
2. **Einstein's Relativity**:
   Time and space are relative, not absolute. Depending on the observer's frame of reference, two people might experience time and distance differently. This aligns with the idea that movement and location are subjective experiences within consciousness.

Thought Experiment: Bringing Reality to You

Try this:

1. **Sit Quietly**: Close your eyes and imagine a distant location—a beach, a mountain, or even another planet.
2. **Visualise**: Instead of picturing yourself travelling there, imagine the location appearing in your awareness.
3. **Feel the Shift**: Notice how the act of visualising brings the destination to you, reinforcing the idea that movement is unnecessary within consciousness.

Ancient Wisdom and Modern Insight

Philosophers and mystics have long suggested that reality is more like a dream or projection than a solid, external construct.

- **The Upanishads** teach that the self (Atman) is not in the world; rather, the world is within the self.
- In **Taoist philosophy**, the universe unfolds naturally, with no need for force or effort. Movement is perceived, but everything remains part of a singular, interconnected whole.

Implications of the Illusion of Movement

If movement is an illusion, it fundamentally changes how we perceive life:

1. **Freedom from Physical Constraints**: Understanding that consciousness doesn't "move" but is already connected to everything

frees us from the illusion that physical distance separates us from what we seek. While we still need to navigate the physical world in our daily lives, this perspective shifts our focus. It reminds us that the true journey isn't about covering miles but about expanding our awareness. Wherever we go, we are already deeply connected to everything, everywhere—a profound truth that can transform how we experience life's journey.

2. **Empowerment in Creation**:
   If experiences and locations arise within consciousness, you have the power to shape and direct your reality. The "world" you experience is a reflection of your inner state.

3. **A Shift in Perception**:
   Life becomes less about getting somewhere and more about recognising that everything you seek is already within you.

Conclusion: The Journey Within

The concept of movement feels intuitive, but when examined through the lens of consciousness, it begins to dissolve. You're not a traveller moving through a fixed world; you're the observer within whom the entire universe arises and unfolds.

This shift in perspective invites you to experience life in a totally different way. Instead of striving to "get somewhere," you can rest in the knowing that everything you desire and every place you wish to be is already present within the infinite field of your awareness.

Takeaways from Chapter 26:

Consciousness doesn't move—it is infinite and already connected to all things. Physical travel is an illusion; it's the mind that perceives movement. This perspective encourages you to live fully in the present, knowing you're already part of everything.

Chapter 27: The Infinite Potential Within—Ancient Wisdom Meets Modern Science

For centuries, ancient philosophers and spiritual traditions have suggested that the universe is a reflection of the self, and that within each of us lies infinite potential. With modern science now echoing these timeless truths, we find ourselves at the intersection of ancient wisdom and cutting-edge discovery.

This chapter explores the profound idea that *you are not in the universe; the universe is inside you*. It's a journey that reveals how consciousness, far from being an isolated phenomenon, contains all the experiences of existence within.

The Universe Within You

The phrase *Tat Tvam Asi*, or "Thou art that," comes from ancient Hindu philosophy. It expresses the idea that you are not separate from the divine or the universe; you are an integral part of it.

Modern science offers an intriguing parallel. The principles of holography suggest that every part of a hologram contains the entire image of the whole. In the same way, each individual consciousness contains the essence of the universe.

Mind-Bending Thought: When you look up at the stars, you're not just observing the universe; you're experiencing a reflection of the infinite potential within yourself.

The Microcosm and the Macrocosm

Ancient philosophies often spoke of the microcosm (the individual) mirroring the macrocosm (the universe). This idea is echoed in various traditions:

- **Hermeticism**: *As above, so below; as within, so without.*
- **Buddhism**: The universe and all its phenomena arise from the mind.

These teachings align with modern findings in quantum physics, where the behaviour of subatomic particles reflects the larger patterns of the cosmos.

The Science of Potential

We've previously discussed that in the realm of quantum mechanics, particles exist in a state of probability, embodying multiple potentials simultaneously until observed. This suggests that reality itself is not fixed but shaped by consciousness.

The same principle applies to your life. Your potential is not limited by external circumstances or past experiences. Every moment contains infinite possibilities, waiting for you to choose and act.

Tapping into Your Infinite Potential

So how do you access this boundless potential? The answer lies in shifting your perspective and aligning with the deeper truths of your being.

1. **Cultivate Awareness**
   Begin by recognising that your thoughts,

emotions, and actions shape your reality. The more aware you become of this process, the more empowered you are to choose your path.

2. **Embrace Stillness**
   In moments of stillness—whether through meditation, nature walks, or quiet reflection—you connect with the infinite awareness that lies beyond the ego. This is where your true potential resides.
3. **Act with Intention**
   Every choice you make sends ripples through the fabric of reality. By acting with clear intention, you align yourself with the life you want to create.

Ancient Wisdom on the Power of Thought

Many spiritual traditions emphasise the transformative power of thought. Marcus Aurelius, the Stoic philosopher, wrote: *The happiness of your life depends upon the quality of your thoughts.*

This insight is more relevant today than ever. Science now shows that your thoughts influence not only your mental state but also your physical health and external circumstances. By mastering your inner dialogue, you unlock the gateway to your infinite potential.

The Role of Imagination

Albert Einstein famously said, *Imagination is more important than knowledge. For knowledge is limited, whereas imagination embraces the entire world.*

Imagination allows you to tap into the infinite possibilities within you. It's the creative force that bridges the gap between the seen and the unseen, turning dreams into reality.

Exercise: Expand Your Vision

- Set aside time each day to visualise your ideal life.
- Imagine every detail vividly, engaging all your senses.
- Feel the emotions of already living that reality.

This practice strengthens your connection to the infinite field of possibilities, making your vision more tangible and achievable.

Embodying the Infinite

Understanding your infinite potential isn't just an intellectual exercise—it's a way of life. When you align with the truth that you are a microcosm of the universe, you begin to live with greater purpose, clarity, and joy.

Key Points:

- You are a reflection of the infinite.
- Your consciousness contains all the possibilities of existence.
- By aligning with this truth, you can create a life that resonates with your highest aspirations.

Conclusion: The Journey Within

The journey to unlock your infinite potential begins within. As you explore the depths of your consciousness and align with the universal truths, you'll discover that you are far more powerful, creative, and connected than you ever imagined.

Takeaways from Chapter 27:

Ancient philosophies align with modern discoveries, revealing that the universe is within you. Consciousness is the source of all creation, containing infinite potential. Embracing this truth empowers you to co-create your reality with intention and awareness.

In the next chapter, we'll explore the concept of vibration in greater depth, delving into how aligning with higher frequencies can transform your life and elevate your experience of reality.

Chapter 28: The Symphony of Vibration—Tuning into Your Highest Frequency

Imagine that life is a grand symphony, with every particle, thought, and emotion vibrating at its own unique note and frequency. The higher the frequency, the more harmonious and abundant your experience becomes. The key to mastering your life is learning to tune your vibration to resonate with the frequencies of love, joy, and abundance.

In this chapter, we'll explore how vibration shapes reality, and how you can elevate your frequency to transform your life.

Everything Is Vibration

At the most fundamental level, everything in the universe is energy vibrating at different frequencies. This includes:

- **Physical Objects**: From rocks to stars, every form of matter vibrates.
- **Emotions**: Love, gratitude, and joy vibrate at higher frequencies, while fear, anger, and resentment vibrate at lower ones.
- **Thoughts**: Positive thoughts resonate with higher frequencies, attracting uplifting experiences.

This vibrational reality explains why you feel drawn to certain people, places, or experiences—they match your current frequency.

The Law of Vibration and Attraction

The **Law of Vibration** underpins the **Law of Attraction**, which states that like attracts like. Your personal vibration acts as a magnet, drawing experiences, opportunities, and people that resonate with your energetic state.

Practical Insight Reminder: If you're consistently focusing on lack or fear, you'll attract more of the same. But when you shift your focus to gratitude, abundance, and love, you align yourself with experiences that match those high frequencies.

How to Raise Your Vibration

1. **Mindfulness and Meditation**
   - Spend time each day in stillness, focusing on your breath and observing your thoughts.
   - This practice quiets the mind and aligns you with the present moment, where your vibration naturally elevates.
2. **Gratitude Practice**
   - As we explored earlier, gratitude is a powerful way to raise your vibration.
   - Begin and end your day by reflecting on what you're grateful for.
3. **High-Vibration Foods**
   - Fresh, plant-based foods nourish your body and elevate your energy.
   - Processed and chemically-laden foods lower your vibration, leaving you feeling sluggish or emotionally drained.
4. **Positive Affirmations**

- Repeat affirmations that resonate with the life you want to create.
- Phrases like *I am abundant*, *I radiate love*, or *I am in harmony with the universe* can reprogram your subconscious mind to align with higher frequencies.

5. **Surround Yourself with High-Vibration People**
   - Spend time with individuals who uplift and inspire you.
   - Distance yourself from energy-draining relationships where possible.

As we've discussed previously sound is a powerful force that resonates through every part of our being, shaping our emotions, health, and overall well-being. The vibrations of sound interact with us on a deep level, creating harmony within and helping to restore balance to both mind and body. Whether through music, chanting, or intentional sound therapy, these vibrations can have transformative effects, promoting healing, clarity, and even abundance.

Sound isn't just a backdrop to life—it's a dynamic energy that connects us to our inner selves and the world around us. By tapping into its power, we can cultivate greater well-being, emotional balance, and alignment with the life we wish to create.

Mind-Bending Fact: Frequency and Form

A fascinating phenomenon known as **cymatics** demonstrates how sound frequencies can shape matter. When specific tones are played through a medium like water or sand, intricate patterns emerge, reflecting the frequency of the sound.

This reveals that vibration not only influences energy but also gives form to the physical world. In a sense, your thoughts and emotions—vibrations in themselves—are constantly shaping your reality.

Living in Tune with the Universe

When you consciously align your vibration with the frequencies of love, abundance, and gratitude, life flows more effortlessly. Challenges become opportunities, and synchronicities appear as if the universe is working in your favour.

Daily Practice for Alignment:

- Begin your day with a simple question: *What frequency am I tuning into today?*
- Choose an intention that aligns with your highest goals and affirm it throughout the day.

Conclusion: Become the Master of Your Frequency

You are a vibrational being in a vibrational universe. By mastering your frequency, you unlock the power to create a life filled with harmony, joy, and abundance.

Takeaways from Chapter 28:

Life is a symphony of vibrations, and your personal frequency shapes your experience. Aligning with higher frequencies brings clarity, joy, and abundance. You can shift your frequency through mindfulness, gratitude, and conscious living.

Chapter 29: Unity with the Source—The Final Realisation

At the heart of every spiritual journey lies one fundamental truth: *you are connected to the source of all existence*. This source—whether you call it God, the Universe, the Infinite, or simply Consciousness—is not something separate from you. It is the essence of who you are, the eternal wellspring from which all life flows.

In this final chapter, we'll explore the ultimate realisation of unity with the source and how it empowers you to live a life of purpose, peace, and profound connection.

The Source: Infinite and Omnipresent

The source is omniscient (all-knowing) and omnipresent (everywhere at once). It exists beyond time, space, and form, yet it manifests in everything—from the stars in the sky to the breath in your lungs.

This means that every experience, every moment, and every thought is an expression of the source. When you truly grasp this, you realise that life is not happening *to* you but *through* you.

The Illusion of Separation

One of the greatest illusions we face is the belief that we are separate from the source. This illusion arises from the ego, which identifies with the physical body, personal history, and individual thoughts.

But when you look beyond the ego, through meditation, mindfulness, or even moments of awe, you glimpse the truth: there is no separation. The same consciousness that animates you also animates the entire universe.

Experiencing Unity

Moments of unity with the source often arise unexpectedly:

- Standing beneath a starlit sky, feeling 'at one' with the cosmos.
- Losing yourself in the beauty of a sunrise, sensing that time has momentarily stopped.
- Experiencing a deep meditative state where the boundaries of self dissolve.

These moments remind you of your true nature as a limitless, eternal being.

Living in Alignment with the Source

Once you recognise your unity with the source, life takes on a new dimension. Challenges become opportunities for growth, relationships deepen, and your sense of purpose becomes clear.

Here's how to live in alignment with this profound truth:

1. **Practice Presence**
   The source is always accessible in the present moment. By grounding yourself in the now, you align with its infinite wisdom and power.
2. **Act from Love and Compassion**
   Love is the highest frequency, the purest expression of the source. When you act from

love—whether toward yourself, others, or the planet—you align with the source's energy.

3. **Trust the Flow**
   Life's events, even the difficult ones, are part of a greater design. Trusting the flow means recognising that everything unfolds in perfect timing, guided by the source's wisdom.

Signs of Unity in Daily Life

As you deepen your connection with the source, you'll begin to notice signs of alignment:

- **Synchronicities**: Coincidences that feel meaningful, as if the universe is sending you messages.
- **Effortless Manifestations**: Desires unfolding naturally, without force or struggle.
- **Inner Peace**: A profound sense of calm, even in the face of challenges.

These signs serve as reminders that you are living in harmony with the source.

The Source as Your True Self

The ultimate realisation is that you are not a fragment of the universe; you *are* the universe. The same creative energy that shaped galaxies flows through you. This realisation dissolves the illusion of limitation and awakens your infinite potential.

Affirmation:
I am one with the source, eternally connected to the infinite wisdom and love that guides all existence.

Practical Exercise: Connecting with the Source

1. **Find a Quiet Space**: Sit comfortably and close your eyes.
2. **Focus on Your Breath**: With each inhale, imagine drawing in the energy of the source.
3. **Feel the Connection**: Visualise yourself as a radiant being of light, connected to the infinite web of existence.
4. **Affirm Your Unity**: Repeat silently or aloud, *I am the source, and the source is me.*

Practising this regularly will deepen your awareness of your connection to the infinite.

Conclusion: Embracing Your Divine Role

The journey of awakening leads to this final truth: you are a divine creator, eternally connected to the source. By embracing this unity, you unlock the power to live a life of boundless love, joy, and purpose.

Your reality is not a random occurrence but a masterpiece you co-create with the infinite. Step into your role as the captain of your own magnificent journey, and let the adventure unfold.

Takeaways from Chapter 29:

You are not separate from the universe—you are an expression of its infinite energy. Unity with the source means understanding that you are both the observer and the creator. Living from this awareness allows you to embrace life with purpose and grace.

Chapter 30: The Great Remembering: Why Anything Exists at All

As a child, I was haunted by a simple yet profound question: Why does anything exist at all? It wasn't enough to know how things worked; I needed to understand the very reason for existence. This question has guided my journey through life, shaping every discovery, insight, and experience. Now, as we reach the conclusion of this book, it's time to explore that question with the depth it deserves.

The Source and the Eternal Why

At the core of existence lies **conscious awareness**, an infinite and all-knowing essence. In its purest form, consciousness is complete—there's nothing it lacks, nothing it needs to learn. Yet, even in this state of perfection, the source holds an inherent desire: to experience.

Why? Because the act of experiencing creates something new. Just as an artist paints not because the canvas needs it but because the act of creation brings something into existence that didn't exist before, so too does the source seek to express and expand itself.

Human Life: The Sharp End of Creation

Enter the human experience. We, as conscious beings, are on the front lines of this grand experiment. We are the explorers, the creators, the ones who push the boundaries of what's possible. But to truly experience the richness of life, we must first forget our true nature.

This is the paradox of existence: to create and discover, we must perceive ourselves as separate from the source, as individuals navigating an external world. This "forgetting" allows us to start anew, much like an artist beginning with a blank canvas, unburdened by previous creations, free to explore uncharted expressions.

Why Forgetting Is Essential:
If we remembered everything—that we are the infinite source of all things—we would lose the sense of wonder, discovery, and growth that comes from learning, struggling, and creating anew.

Life as a Journey of Discovery and Creativity

Life, then, is a journey back to remembering. Along the way, we experience the full spectrum of existence: joy and sorrow, love and loss, creation and destruction. Each moment, no matter how ordinary or extraordinary, adds to the collective tapestry of the universe.

1. **The Power of Contrast**:
   We come to understand light because we've experienced darkness. We cherish love because we've felt loss. These contrasts enrich the source's understanding and add depth to its infinite being.
2. **The Role of Creativity**:
   Every thought, invention, and act of kindness contributes to the ever-expanding universe. We are not passive observers; we are active participants in the unfolding story of existence.

The Answer Lies in the Experience

So, why does anything exist at all? Because through existence, consciousness experiences itself. The universe is not a random, chaotic event—it is a masterpiece in progress, an infinite symphony where every note matters.

Your life, in all its uniqueness, is a vital part of that symphony. Every choice you make, every experience you have, adds to the richness of the source. You are the universe in motion, exploring itself, creating itself, and ultimately, remembering itself.

The Childlike Wonder

In the end, we return to the childlike state of wonder, not as naïve beings but as enlightened creators. We remember that life isn't about reaching a destination but about experiencing the journey. And in that journey, we find our purpose: to create, to love, and to be the source's eyes, ears, and hands in this ever-expanding universe.

So, the next time you ponder why anything exists at all, remember: you are both the question and the answer, the explorer and the creator, the child and the infinite.

Conclusion: Embracing the Infinite Journey

Life is not about escaping its challenges or accumulating material wealth—it's about experiencing everything, from the mundane to the miraculous. It's about deep connections, moments of awe, and the courage to create something new.

And as you move forward, remember this: you are the source, experiencing itself through the unique lens of your life. Embrace the journey, for in doing so, you fulfil the greatest purpose of all.

Takeaways from Chapter 30:

Life exists as a journey of discovery and creation, driven by the source's desire to experience itself. Forgetting our divine origin allows us to live fresh, authentic human experiences. Remembering who we truly are—consciousness itself—is an integral part of life's journey. It's a process of reassembling, starting with the smallest perceptions and understandings, and expanding toward the vast, infinite source of everything.

Chapter 31: Rise and Shine—It's Time to Wake Up

You've journeyed through the mysteries of consciousness, explored the vast expanse of the multiverse, and learned how your thoughts, intentions, and actions shape your reality. Now, it's time to step fully into your power as a conscious creator. The awakening you've begun is not the end; it's the beginning of a life lived with purpose, clarity, and boundless potential.

Awakening to Your Power

Every moment of your life has led to this point. The challenges, the triumphs, the doubts, and the revelations—they've all been pieces of a larger puzzle, guiding you toward the truth: You are not a passive observer of life; you are its creator.

This realisation is both liberating and empowering. It means that you have the ability to shape your reality, to rise above limitations, and to align your life with your deepest desires. No longer are you confined by the stories of the past or the expectations of others. You are free to write your own narrative, one that reflects the infinite potential of your true self.

From Awakening to Action

Awakening is only the first step. To fully embody your power, you must move from awareness to action. This requires clarity of intention, trust in the process, and the courage to act in alignment with your highest self.

Here are some practical steps to integrate your awakening into daily life:

Set Intentions Daily
Begin each day by consciously setting your intentions. Whether it's to approach your work with creativity, strengthen your relationships, or find moments of joy, clear intentions help you align your actions with your desires.

Practice Presence
Life unfolds in the present moment. By cultivating mindfulness, you anchor yourself in the now, where your true power lies. Presence allows you to respond to life with clarity and wisdom rather than reacting from fear or habit.

Embrace Challenges as Opportunities
Every obstacle is a chance for growth. When faced with difficulties, ask yourself, What is this teaching me? How can I use this experience to evolve? Shifting your perspective transforms challenges into stepping stones.

Celebrate Small Wins
Progress isn't always dramatic. Celebrate every step forward, no matter how small. These moments of recognition reinforce your commitment and build momentum toward your larger goals.

Shining Your Light

As you step into your role as a conscious creator, you naturally begin to radiate a higher vibrational energy. This light not only transforms your life but also touches those around you. You become a beacon of possibility, inspiring others to awaken to their own power.

This isn't about preaching or forcing change; it's about living authentically and allowing your actions to speak louder than words. When you embody love, courage, and purpose, you invite others to do the same.

The Ripple Effect

Your journey of awakening creates a ripple effect that extends far beyond your immediate circle. As you align with your true self and manifest your desires, you contribute to the collective evolution of humanity. Each act of kindness, each moment of gratitude, each conscious choice adds to the growing wave of positive change in the world.

Imagine a world where more people awaken to their power, where love and compassion replace fear and division. Your light is a vital part of this transformation.

A New Reality Awaits

As you turn the last page of this book, know that the journey never ends. It's a lifelong process of awakening, exploring, creating and expanding. Trust in your path, stay connected to the source, and remember: you are the universe experiencing itself in human form.

The power to shape your reality is in your hands. Wake up to the limitless potential within you, and step boldly into the magnificent life that awaits. The universe is ready to co-create with you. The question is: Are you now ready to rise and shine?

-Authors Recommended Reading

Exploring the depths of consciousness and personal transformation can be greatly enhanced by engaging with the works of renowned authors in the field. Here is a curated list of influential books that offer diverse perspectives and insights:

The Power of Now - by Eckhart Tolle

This seminal work guides readers towards spiritual enlightenment by emphasising the importance of living fully in the present moment.

Conversations with God - by Neale Donald Walsch

Presented as a dialogue between the author and the divine, this book explores profound spiritual questions and offers insights into life's purpose and meaning.

You Are the Universe - by Deepak Chopra

Co-authored with physicist Menas Kafatos, this book delves into the connection between human consciousness and the cosmos, proposing that individuals are integral to the universe's unfolding.

Slay Your Dragons with Compassion - by Malcolm Stern

Drawing from his experience as a psychotherapist, Stern provides tools for navigating personal challenges, emphasising the power of compassion and connection.

Becoming Supernatural: How Common People Are Doing the Uncommon - by Dr. Joe Dispenza

Combining scientific research with practical exercises, Dispenza demonstrates how individuals can transcend limitations and achieve extraordinary states of being.

Additionally, the following recommended books are available on Audible, offering accessible audio formats for immersive learning:

A New Earth: Awakening to Your Life's Purpose - by Eckhart Tolle

This follow-up to "The Power of Now" explores the structure of the human ego and its impact on personal happiness, guiding readers towards a higher state of consciousness.

The Untethered Soul: The Journey Beyond Yourself - by Michael A. Singer

Singer examines the concept of self and the inner dialogue that often limits personal growth, offering insights into achieving inner freedom.

The Art of Loving - by Erich Fromm

A classic work that explores love as an active art, requiring knowledge and effort, and discusses its role in human relationships and self-fulfilment.

Engaging with these texts can provide valuable perspectives and practical guidance on the journey towards self-discovery and personal transformation.

Contact the author beyondreality800@gmail.com

Printed in Great Britain
by Amazon

55580223R00106